Spatial Ecologies

Urban Sites, State and World-Space
in French Cultural Theory

T0311307

Contemporary French and Francophone Cultures 21

Contemporary French and Francophone Cultures

This series aims to provide a forum for new research on modern and contemporary French and francophone cultures and writing. The books published in *Contemporary French and Francophone Cultures* reflect a wide variety of critical practices and theoretical approaches, in harmony with the intellectual, cultural and social developments which have taken place over the past few decades. All manifestations of contemporary French and francophone culture and expression are considered, including literature, cinema, popular culture, theory. The volumes in the series will participate in the wider debate on key aspects of contemporary culture.

Recent titles in the series:

VERENA ANDERMATT CONLEY

Spatial Ecologies
Urban Sites, State and World-Space in French Cultural Theory

LIVERPOOL UNIVERSITY PRESS

First published 2012 by
Liverpool University Press
4 Cambridge Street
Liverpool
L69 7ZU

This paperback version published 2014

British Library Cataloguing-in-Publication data
A British Library CIP record is available

ISBN 978-1-84631-754-5 cased
978-1-78138-005-5 paperback

Typeset by XL Publishing Services, Exmouth
Printed and bound by CPI Group (UK), Croydon CR0 4YY

For Tom,
my spatial companion

Contents

Introduction
Space as a Critical Concept

This book moves along the wide arc of the "spatial turn" that critical thinking has taken over the last thirty years. It follows this trajectory in order to see how and where *space*, something that defies reduction to a simple or stable definition, can now be appreciated for its ecological implications. The principal argument that follows is that, to varying degrees, philosophers born of or nurtured by the ferment of "May 1968" build their work over a spatial crisis that has since broadened to include consideration of the well-being of the planet. When critics and writers take a spatial turn they move from traditionally restricted fields of study, their disciplines as it were, to see where their work stands in view of globalization. The spatial turn now curves toward an ethics of living and working collectively on a planet whose habitability seems to be problematic and whose resources are today less abundant than they had been three decades ago.

Before all else it must be asked: might a prodigiously accumulating critical mass of writing on space be a symptom of a diminishing return?[1] Would the increasing number of reflections on the nature of space betray a sense of its attrition? The questions are posed to underscore the paradox motivating much of what follows. While the space our globe allots to us can seem oddly infinite in its finite measure, our worst fears tell us that it is vanishing. But how do we perceive—how do we experience—space so that we may know what it is and appreciate it for what it may be? Before responding to this second question we realize that its formulation tells us that we must have a physical sense of space prior to seeking a definition of its essence. Contrary to the order of classical philosophy, our *apprehension* of space, the basis for its epistemology, precedes its ontology. The very being of space can only be discerned by how we sense it and by what we feel we know of it. What we ascertain about it is gauged by the way we feel it dilating, contracting, folding upon itself and

---

1 Included are a watershed volume edited by Mike Crang and Nigel Thrift, *Thinking Space* (2000), David Harvey's numerous books since the *Condition of Postmodernity* (1991), which have appeared at regular intervals (2000, 2006, 2009a, 2009b), and a host of others, beginning with Edward Soja, that are generally affiliated with Henri Lefebvre.

extending in our midst. We generally tend to define space in the spirit of analogy or relation, especially in the connection between space and place. Perception of the latter can prompt cognizance of the former, and vice-versa. Place is simply *there*, while space is produced or *invented*. The former is gained through the transformation of the latter, and so on.[2]

We can begin to think of space by paraphrasing Rousseau's famous incipit to the *Social Contract*: everywhere we live in space, but everywhere it wastes away. Because space is perceived and understood in the context of place, we are urged to learn to look at it only contextually or as a function of what inhabits it. We are informed of its compression and, as a result, of issues in the world at large that range from social contradiction—the abysmal gap between haves and have-nots—to the uneven economic development we witness everywhere around us. Utopian philosophers claim that it is vital for us to invent new spaces. What might this generalized creation of space look like, and what does the term mean once its "turn" is shown bending in the direction of a political ecology? In the pages that follow the aim is to cast a critical gaze on the legacy of space as it has been elaborated in French theory, specifically from the 1960s to today. I will identify various types of space and see how the term replaces or complements *time*, what had been from Descartes to Sartre the bedrock of the French existential heritage, as an operative critical concept. Without requisite allusion to David Harvey, Edward Soja and others who inherit and craft their observations under the formula, I will locate (or, by way of paradox, set in place) the spatial turn in French theory and then inquire of its validity today, when interrelated political and infrastructural dilemmas beset an increasingly urbanized planet. I will limit the concept historically and geographically to France, where theory has been astonishingly productive, to ask if and how, today, we can *negotiate* and *translate* this concept productively in the critical spheres in which we live. In other words what use can we make of the heritage of space as a critical concept?

A prefatory interlude: in my childhood I got lost in space. Growing up in Switzerland, in a post-Second World War environment where the Cold War seemed to freeze time in the wake of the horrendous events of the 1940s, I was perhaps not really "lost" in space, nor was I, like many

2   Two cardinal points of reference for this study are, first, from the standpoint of philosophy, Edward Casey's *Fate of Place* (1997) and, tellingly, a sequel, *Representing Place* (2002); secondly, Michel de Certeau's contention, in *The Practice of Everyday Life* (1984), that *space*, felt through an active, discursive relation with the world at large, transforms its passive, often inert and silent counterpoint of *place*.

others, living in the aura of existential alienation. The child that I believe I was may have felt an acute sense of enclosure in a landlocked nation whose infinite *outside* could only be fathomed in the imagination of what extended over the peaks of its high mountains. An enclosure that inhered (literally) *in here* spurred a desire to see and live the world *out there*, outside of the perimeters of the politically "neutral" landscape of Switzerland into which I had been born. In retrospect, my yearning for wide-open spaces, like those of the America I had romanticized, was most likely a reaction to something more than what many would like to call the malaise of those living in a small, landlocked nation: a geographical compression. The feeling might have been in response, more broadly, to symbolic orders based on traditional authority and on state institutions, in other words to what Michel Foucault would soon call the "disciplinary" society that still had currency in post-war Europe. My yearning to go anywhere out of this world led me to devour travel narratives and gaze upon glossy pages in the *National Geographic* where deserts, plains and oceans invited the imagination to unfold and wander along the shorelines and into the vast landscapes of the east and the west. I dreamt of other spaces through pictures and their legends long before physically crossing the Atlantic by boat, the voyage taking place on the cusp of the moment when, with the expansion of air travel, the great and not-so-great ocean liners were being hoisted into dry dock or shaped into harborside restaurants.

Space was suddenly felt to be "incredibly shrinking" under the impact of accelerated modes of transportation. Now, several decades later, these recollections of two modes of transport, the ocean liner and the propeller-driven airplane, seem to belong to a collective memory bank. Sparked by novelists and playwrights, I felt at the same time an ecstatic rush of "liberation" that later, in an intellectual way, I perceived as having to do with a growing sense of the loss of "traditional" modes of existence. Yet I soon defined the character of this shrinkage as a growing compression of urbanized space and time in view of what I experienced in the crowded subways of New York and in airplanes stuffed with passengers. The open vistas of the pictures I so admired in my childhood lost their gloss. I found myself growing into a reduced world under the spell of technology, uneven development and consumerism yet while continuing to harbor the vital illusion that this very compression might also bring with it possibilities or, in other words, new spatial openings.

It was thus by elective affinity that I happened upon French theorists from the 1960s whose interests, each in different ways and to varying degrees, seemed to share common foci. In their lapidary brilliance they conceptualized what I had lived confusedly as a child. A decade after Claude Lévi-Strauss's melancholy drift about the exploitation of Brazil and the waning of the planet in *Tristes tropiques* (1955), a study that contemplated the world "cooling" under the force of entropy, these French theorists configured space in reaction to what only later would I qualify as a nagging feeling about transformation: transformations wrought by the state, imparted by the capital of technology, giving rise to economic shifts and, no less, the new geographies of migration and increasing density of population. After locating these transformations in the wake of the "disciplining power of the state," some (but not all) of the same critical and cultural theorists gradually came to realize that, now far from 1968, they were dealing with an entirely new state of things. What had first been perceived to be an intensification of "discipline" that the state imposed on its "subjects" was due, in fact, to the advent of these transformations. It was also the threshold at which became noticeable what now goes by the name of "globalization," that is, what might be imagined as an electro-economic wiring and almost cybernetic management of the world. From the angle of the history of critical theory the onset of globalization that the media aggressively reports to have been made possible by "new" electronic technologies has led—and here is the principal drift of this book—to an informed discovery of space in French theory.

It dawned upon me that my confused, rebellious discovery came at the very moment when space was becoming, in France anyway, a privileged object of study. The purportedly "spatial turn" was a symptom of the transformation of a guiding concept into which these new mentors had been born. An inherited idea of space as being stable, either bounded or boundless, was disappearing. What I had felt in childhood and adolescence acquired an unsettling and darkened aura. The "I" who had this experience was collective; the "I" who would suffuse its writing with the first-person singular was the mirage of a subject-position. Further reflection needed to be made in a singular *and* a plural voice.

Over the last four decades, space has become one of the more commonly discussed concepts in fields ranging from critical and cultural theory to anthropology and sociology, no longer addressed solely by geography, but also in architecture, urban studies and ecology. In North America, many of those who write about space are indebted to the same panoply of French theorists. While they understand it in different ways, they all concur with what Michel Serres remarked in his *Natural Contract*: space no longer simply serves as a setting in which heroic human beings move about. In contrast to *place*, space is variously seen as a production, an invention, an opening, an area in-between, interme-diary, a continuum in perpetual transition. While critics of culture acknowledge a debt to French theorists, they tend to think of space in a general and rather universal fashion without referring back to the condi-tions of its elaboration. In this book, the heritage and the conceptual virtue of space in French cultural and critical theory are paramount.

The method is at once historical and diagrammatic. I shall pursue a fairly close reading of works of theorists whose virtues come forward when they are placed along a historical axis and in juxtaposition to one another. From each angle—one in relation to the force of theory in 1968 and the other by way of the places they occupy in respect to each other—a sense of a broader picture will emerge. I will set aside the literary space that writers-philosophers (perhaps a mutant species born of the turmoil of the 1960s) such as Maurice Blanchot, Jacques Derrida, Hélène Cixous and others have developed in favor of gaining a greater purchase on topics that include urbanization, the transformation of the nation-state, consumerism, demography and the onset of globalization. In his *French Theory* (2008) François Cusset, spiritual child of the generation of 1968, acknowledges that the philosophical and political work of his forebears has utterly changed the ways in which we live in the world. France in the context of the 1960s had a unique profile. The country's historical, social and geographical condition led to a revolt of students who allied—yes—with *workers* to contest the dictates of Gaullist policy emanating from the Elysée Palace. The moment witnessed the onset of massive migra-tions, first as a consequence of decolonization (which was tied to globalization, still referred to as "Americanization" and thought of as a direct consequence of the Marshall Plan), rapid urbanization and, of importance to this study, a sense of the loss of myriad physical, symbolic and mental spaces. This sea change might not have been possible without the unforeseen force and drive of the theorists' speech and writing. Most theories devised in the 1960s, and often overtly written in the wake of Freud and Marx, were highly politicized. As we can read in Cusset's polemical history, this politicization has disappeared in France and since migrated to other places and been redrawn in different idioms for different ends. It is thus all the more compelling to work through the major theorists to see not only how they think about space but also how the concepts shaping it evolve over time and what, if legacies there are, can be translated and negotiated today, at a time when our world faces major political and ecological dilemmas that many still refuse to acknowledge. The writers and philosophers taken up here all share a sense of the precariousness of our condition and, when they are seen in the rearview mirror of this study, they allow us to move forward with fresh and keen conviction.

In *Ecopolitics*, to which this study has been written (albeit unconsciously) as an open-ended sequel, I focused on a repressed ecological dimension in French theory wherever it drew a bead on the concept and invention of *nature*.[3] In this project I want to focus on space in relation to ecology in the sense of a domestication of the *oikos* or of ways of exchanging in and with the world as it is developed through questions of making habitable or of living well in milieus in which it is not easy to do so. Many works discussed here underline the importance of ecology in relation to *habitus* and especially to habitability. *Habitus*, an expression coined by Marcel Mauss in 1936 and reshaped later by Lévi-Strauss and others, serves the end of analyzing how structures determine practices. With its many synonyms such as *ethos* or *exis* it refers to a set of practices within a given social matrix. Theorists from Alexandre Kojève to Henri Lefebvre and from Pierre Bourdieu to Michel de Certeau have adopted it in various ways. For Mauss, *habitus* is a convention established by reigning cultural discourses, of which individual speech is an extension. While critics such as Bourdieu believed that *habitus* is limited and even determined by social structures, those such as Lefebvre, Certeau and the others who take center stage in the pages that follow look for the creation of openings in and from *habitus*.

To *make habitable*, in turn, has at least distant echoes of Martin Heidegger who in a lecture given in 1951 discussed dwelling in relation to space in existential terms. His was a time of rapid transformation wrought by instrumental technologies brought forward in the post-Second World War era. A space, the philosopher declares, is "that for which room has been made, that which is let into its bounds" (1993: 356). He makes a distinction between this kind of space as *Raum* and another that consists of mere intervals or dimensions. Heidegger is preoccupied with tracing in "thought the essence of dwelling" (363). Only when we are thus capable of dwelling, he asserts, can we build—and by building we gather that he implies picturing and imagining. He gives the example of an eighteenth-century farmhouse in the Black Forest as a perfect dwelling. There he finds that earth and sky, divinities and mortals enter into a *simple oneness* that orders the house (362, author's

---

3 Carolyn Merchant's groundbreaking work, *The Death of Nature* (1978), preceded by Gregory Bateson's *Steps Toward an Ecology of Mind* (1972), counted among the works of Anglo-Saxon origin that were displaced into the context of French theory.

emphasis). Inquiring about the state of dwelling in his "precarious age" (363), he notes that its absence is not simply related to a material lack but to the absence of an existential dimension. While few of the theorists discussed here will clamor for the kind of rustic oneness Heidegger favored, they make strident appeals for the opening of a space that would not be purely interval or dimension but where habitability would be defined in clearly existential and ecological terms. How, they ask, can we produce an ecologically viable space that makes the world habitable not simply through the fantasy of a return to a rustic way of living on a generally urbanized planet? Though the meaning of *making habitable* changes from one author to the next, the expression always refers to an existential way of being and of living in the world, or of opening ecological spaces that, as Félix Guattari puts it, can be mental, social or natural. At times, "habitable" emphasizes a non-alienated, unified way of being (as in Henri Lefebvre). At others, it is used in the sense of rendering the world habitable for human projects by thinking and acting in sustainable, ecological ways (as in Félix Guattari). It refers also to the opening of a vital "breathing" space between networks (as in Bruno Latour or even in Gilles Deleuze and Félix Guattari). Over the decades, tension accrues between existential and political spheres in a networked world where subjects must gain spatial consciousness in thinking of themselves both as individuals and as *citizens* in a global polis (as in Etienne Balibar).

Though their theories were at first meant to carry universal significance, the same critics become more and more aware of their new status in a world where the axis "Paris and the rest of the world," or center and periphery, has little currency and where competing universalities cause them to continually reassess the worth of their projects. As Marc Augé has noted, the world of techno-economic globalization is one of passage and circulation driven by consumption. From concepts of space in which consumption and electronic networking play a strong role, a common urgency emerges from the writings of a select group of critics. It has to do with the dilemmas that come with the transformation of a world inherited from the modernist, industrial and colonial traditions and of the growth of another that knows no borders, a world that, perhaps because we now call it global, makes manifest its fragility.

These writers address an ecological urgency in the emphasis they place on producing, constructing and opening spaces so as to enable and assure a dynamic equilibrium of habitability. Where and how the stress is distributed depends on the aims, the reach, or even the geographies of their fields of study, which, perhaps as good fortune would have it, are increasingly hybridized. It also depends to a considerable measure on the date and place of the writings as well as on individual, cultural and political situations unique to their work. In retrospect, however, we can see that while all of them sense an impending globalization of the world's economy, yoked to a transition from an industrial age to one of information, the earlier theorists of space emphasize more the relation of the subject to the disciplinary state. Later generations of critics address the economic shift to consumerism and the accompanying loss of reference to the world at large before focusing on the impact of electronic networks as well as of problems of migration. They all analyze space in relation to a city, changing from a somewhat enclosed entity to an amorphous sprawl and, further, to a generalized urban condition. They attend to rapid alterations of the nation-state while also considering the increasing mediation between humans and machines in a transnational arena.

The common emphasis is increasingly on the emergence of a world whose welter of subjectivities and time-space coordinates bears little resemblance to the economic or physical geographies inherited from the era that saw the beginnings of oceanic travel, nor even, with regard to the coordinates of this study, to the decade of the 1960s. All these writers, critical of the repressions and domination wrought by capital, argue continuously and vigorously for the necessity of inventing new spaces that are at once grounded *and* utopian, real *and* fictional, theoretical *and* practical. As many of these critics claim, a "utopian" element is necessary for the invention of a new space, and the production of a so-called real is always in part "fictional." The real, as Etienne Balibar would have it, is what is produced from experience and a *locus of fiction*—or a fictional site—at the intersection of historical, geographical and symbolic (and unconscious) conditions.

The fictions these theorists craft all bear a strong signature of the 1960s, yet they evolve over the next four decades, after 1989 and especially since 2001, from a preoccupation with "vanishing" existential spaces to a coming to terms with existing in a networked, diverse, multipolar and densely populated world. The ordering of the chapters in this book reflects the individual differences among these French theorists while suggesting, as each gives way to the next, an evolution of the very concept of space. I count Henri Lefebvre and Michel de Certeau among the existential avatars of the new spatial turn, and consider Jean Baudrillard to be a brilliantly annoying *agon* and magus of spatial theory in the world of media. Marc Augé is shown following the footsteps of Certeau's narrators of spatial stories before leading us into a realm of non-places, the very sites that define what he calls super-modernity. At an axis of these reflections stands Paul Virilio, who in my opinion remains at once a highly existential thinker while being nonetheless cognizant (perhaps via a creative paranoia that gives rise to his concept of deadly premonition) of spatial and ecological catastrophes in our midst. Likewise, but with strident resonance, Gilles Deleuze and Félix Guattari borrow from Virilio the concept of *territorialization* to find an ecology of mind and body (much like that of their mentor Gregory Bateson) in milieus where space is very limited. Their work resonates with Bruno Latour, the historian and philosopher of science who espouses the cause of networks and asks how we are to exist on a fully urbanized planet Earth. Finally, I would like to yoke spatial theory to the concept of the subject and the citizen insofar as it goes with Etienne Balibar's political writings on the necessity of constructing a new space for "democracy" in a global age.

Though I touch on literature and film, as I have stated above, I do not include works that deal with literary space per se such as those written in the lineage of Maurice Blanchot's *Espace litteraire* (1955; Eng. trans. *The Space of Literature*, 1986) or with related philosophical reflections, à la Jacques Derrida, that introduce time in space. Allusion will be made to them when pertinent. I choose the theorists noted above because of their common focus and the implications of their work for the future— because they all ask how the world can be made habitable and, we can hope, viable. Finally, when discussing the future of space or future ecological spaces, I would like to see what we can lift from these theories today, when we stand on the threshold of collective management (or collective and regional resistance to management) of space vital to the future of the planet. As Félix Guattari wrote almost three decades ago, science does not hang on to concepts that are assumed to be immutable. Theoretical concepts are tools. What, if anything, can we lift from these theories produced in what Guattari would call the "toolbox" of the 1960s, a decade known for its strong belief in a viable tomorrow? What do these tools allow us to do, and how can they be useful for what must be done today in order to open ecological spaces and make habitable the world in which we live? If *habitable* once meant access to a non-alienated way of living the everyday, far from state control and other forms of power, how can we think of it in relation to space at a time when many people do not have access to the experience of an everyday life, understood as a practice not based entirely on subsistence or survival nor so destitute as to be devoid of common and collective symbolic activities? Where do we carve open sites that allow the insertion of the pleasures of living *tout court*? The habitable of today can no longer be thought separately from natural and manufactured resources. While in a networked world it is of continued importance to hold to an existential dimension for the construction of ecological space, the latter cannot be thought without increased attention to pressing concrete issues. The problems have intensified and accelerated over the decades. They are singular but also collective in every practical sense. The pages that follow will, hopefully, pose these questions while seeking and evaluating answers from French theorists at the leading edge of the spatial turn of the 1960s and beyond.

1

Henri Lefebvre: Lived Spaces

Space is only a medium, environment and means, an instrument and intermediary [...] [It] never possesses existence in itself but always refers to
something else, to existential and simultaneously essential time, subjective
and objective [...]

Lefebvre, *The Urban Revolution*

The user's space is lived not represented (or conceived).
Lefebvre, *The Production of Space*

Immense credit is due to Henri Lefebvre for having inaugurated new itineraries of inquiry in critical and cultural theory in the aftermath of the
Second World War. Enduring achievements are found in all of his myriad
writings, but nowhere more than in his watershed *Production of Space*
(1974), a monumental study in which he asserts that after the turmoil of
1968 a renewed awareness of space complicates inherited ways of calcu-
lating time. Space is no longer a neutral background against which
humans move about, but is what humans *produce* as, in turn, it shapes
or even produces them. It is both a medium in which things are fashioned
and a milieu in which they find their place. Lefebvre correlatively offers
a theory and a history of contemporary space coordinated according to
the effects of uneven economic development, the advent of the modern
State (generally in upper case), and the impact of the accelerated circulation of capital in the bourgeois sphere during the "Trente Glorieuses"
or three decades of prosperity that France witnessed after 1945.

He argues that those in power, together with those in collusion with
governmental agencies, impose spatial constraints that regiment the lived
experience of entire populations. Acutely aware of the Cold War as a
time of intense transformation, early on Lefebvre foresees an impending
globalization that under the impact of consumer capitalism will displace
industrial society from its basis in the manufacture of objects to the
commerce of information. He calls into question the heroic Marxist
efforts aimed at unifying the world that finished in the gulag, and the
longer-lasting effect of the totalitarian state. More traditional (and, as
his use of "tradition" implies, "slower" and more deliberate) ways of
using space are jettisoned where signs take the place of things. Because

11

they define their lives through the ways they handle and exchange their "things" while living within a regime of signs, humans become increasingly alienated from their bodies and their ties to the world. However (Lefebvre continually asserts), each order brings with it new possibilities for coping with alienation (or reinventing space), and thus it becomes the philosopher's task to raise collective awareness of the transformations under way and to allow new possibilities of invention to emerge. Echoing the feminist slogan of the time, Lefebvre wants us to have "our bodies, our selves" become one and the same.

Marked by a host of intellectual and artistic movements—surrealism, phenomenology, existentialism, situationism and even structuralism as well as post-structuralism—Lefebvre treats space in respect of their vision and ideology, yet when all is said and done he reads the world through a Marxian lens. He openly borrows from various philosophers including Bachelard, Heidegger, Nietzsche and Spinoza. He occasionally refers to Gilles Deleuze, Michel Foucault, Julia Kristeva and Jacques Derrida.[1] In staunchly Marxian terms he asks how a power elite driven by capital, itself inseparable from the technologies that fashion its current process, shapes the lives of the people under its jurisdiction. There are those who produce space and those who are made to practice and live it according to the design of whoever is in power—be they politicians, urbanists or architects.

He countenances the waning of the core of an industrial society, that which had stood at the endpoint of the inherited periodization of history according to Marxian chronology. Urbanization is key to the advent of a *spatial turn*, the exact paradigm of which, he insists, is yet to be determined. This new urban society does not function according to a notion of time equated with progress, a concept basic to industrial capitalism. In addition to disengaging a paradigm shift from industrial to urban society and from time to space, Lefebvre asks two pressing questions: what exactly are the spaces that those in power impose, and what are the *other* spaces that can be invented through acts of resistance to overcome alienation? With the impact of consumer capitalism driven by commercial implementation of new technologies, "lethal" signs begin to proliferate and oppress growing numbers of people while, at the same time, the undoing of fixed or fixing symbols (which keep people "in their place") sets the stage for spatial invention. It is more important than ever,

---

1 Lefebvre attacks structuralist and post-structuralist theorists from Claude Lévi-Strauss to Michel Foucault who, he argues, conflate real and mental space when they overemphasize language and discourse at the price of lived experience. He lauds other thinkers, among them Jacques Derrida and Julia Kristeva, for retaining a notion of corporality and of bodily rhythms.

he argues, to conceive spaces free of controlling symbols, which will indeed be *habitable*. The transformations Lefebvre sees under way in post-war France reinforce the separation between abstract and concrete things, between signs and lived experience. At the same time they make possible a reordering of space that in the best of conditions might lead to less alienated ways of living in the world. The philosopher's task is to transform the idle, the unemployed and the passive consumer into creative producers.

Lived Spaces and the Re-creation of Everyday Life

Lefebvre's observations about the character of contemporary space and how it can be produced in new ways are informed by a variegated history. How and why he eventually takes a spatial turn can be seen in the rich and often "uneven" development of his thinking in its movement from its topographical orientation to a vision of global space. Published in French in 1947 (hence at the beginning of the three decades of prosperity in France), the first volume of *Critique of Everyday Life* stands as a prelude to his work of 1974. Lefbvre focuses on lived spaces and the everyday, which he finds in their purest form in the country, in which the everyday is synonymous with a common experience of biological life, indeed its pulsation and sensation, felt in the body prior to its translation into signs. Taking note of the progressive erasure of the demarcation between life and the signs that replace or reify it, he finds solace in the country while at the same time undoing the myth of pastoral ways of living that would be opposed to a degraded life in the city. Much in the way of Raymond Williams in *The Country and the City* (1999), Lefebvre notes that the rural world, however much it speaks to our romantic longings, is rife with political and especially religious repressions. Paradoxically, urbanization is what tends to mitigate the nefarious effects of religion. Yet because it is tied to urbanization, bourgeois capitalism, itself cloaked under religious piety, imposes new constraints by means of technologies and consumerism, two master causes of uneven economic and spatial development. Analyzing the "backward sector" of the everyday, Lefebvre examines how bodies incorporate, unbeknownst to themselves, "official" ideas and concepts of space in their "most concrete condition." A critique of the everyday and a reinvention of lived space, he hopes, will reconcile thought *and* life or thought *and* action.[2] We must

2 On this point see especially Trebitsch (1991: ix–xxviii).

be active practitioners in order that, whether in the country or the city, the everyday can become a creative milieu or a continuum in which living can be developed into an "art" available to an anonymous collectivity. The aim is to make thought "intervene in life in its humblest details" so as "to change life [and] lucidly to recreate everyday life" (1991a: 227). Vast numbers of people, especially city-dwellers, have strayed too far from simple existential truths. When people stroll through the country-side, Lefebvre writes, in the manner of Rousseau's solitary *promeneur*, presumably walking on the outskirts of Geneva,

> [t]hey do not know how to see this reality, so near and so vast, these forms creative [human] labor has produced. City dwellers getting away from it all, intellectuals at a loose end, we wander through the French countryside simply for something to do, we look but we are unable to see [...] We fail to see the [human] facts where they are, namely in humble, familiar, everyday objects: the shape of fields, of ploughs. Our search for the human takes us too far, too "deep." We seek it in the clouds or in mysteries, whereas it is waiting for us, besieging us on all sides. We will not find it in myths—although human facts carry with them a long and magnificent procession of legends, tales and songs, poems and dances. All we need do is simply to open our eyes, to leave the dark world of metaphysics and the false depths of the "inner life" behind, and we will discover the immense human wealth that the humblest facts of everyday life contain. (1991a: 132).

In the same *Critique* Lefebvre describes what he calls more traditional conditions of living based on harmony of humans and nature. Nature is never a brute state of things but rather a force of awareness or conscious-ness that comes forward through the art of active and creative human intervention. Alienation appears with progressive abstraction, which results from a slow but inescapable separation of humans from the envi-ronment that nourishes them. With the rise of industrial capitalism, the process by which things are turned into coefficients of worth (use-value and exchange-value) abets separation and promotes a loss of dynamic harmony. Where signs quantify "input" and "output" they divide man from nature and cause human action to lose its living substance. As a result "everyday life" becomes visibly degraded. Yet even if it is proof of alienation, it is also, for Lefebvre, the remainder in and through which actions can produce something new.

While in other sectors of France science and consciousness have progressed, Lefebvre concludes, in the rural areas "innocent life" can be found in a "degraded" and "humiliated" condition. The village "huddles around its dead" where religious rituals have been "hideously commer-cialized" (1991a: 210). Though life in the country remains more cyclical and obeys slower rhythms of circulation, it too concedes to commer-cialism. The rural world is a space where debilitating political and religious strictures are lived canonically and without question. In a "Notes Written One Sunday in the French Countryside," Lefebvre writes upon revisiting the parish church of his childhood, "I hesitate on its humble, unadorned threshold, held back by a kind of apprehension. I know what I shall find: an empty, echoing space with hidden recesses crammed with hundreds of objects, each uttering the silent cry that makes it a sign. What a strange power!" (1991a: 213). He adds:

> And I know that [my] suppressed anger is another aspect of the power, the nascent fascination of the "sacred" object. It is impossible to free myself from it. For me this space can never be just like any other space. But precisely because I feel this obscure emotion I can begin to understand its obscure causes. So I must not despair, the fight goes on...

He concludes what clearly seems to be a psychomachia in which conflicting points of view are staged in the dialogue he leads with himself: "In this way the illusion by which religion deceives us (that vain and ever-broken promise of community, of the power to act) tends to be born again with every action in our everyday lives and prevents us from living" (1991a: 214). In the cool and dank air that smells of mortar and stone he feels that beneath the vaulted nave he hears the echoes of religious ritual in a bygone space that nonetheless holds him in its grip. Lived spaces have to be free of such constraints. Just as harmonies of space and time are felt more vividly in the country, an oppressive past, indeed a mental space of millennial duration, casts oppressive shadows upon him. Where he had sought relief from urban stress he finds religion. And, worse than the opiate it had been for Marx, the sensation of religion that darkens his day in the country reminds him that organized belief "accumulates all man's helplessness. It offers a critique of life: it is itself that critique: a reactionary, destructive critique" (1991a: 227) that, building its economy on death, like capitalism, drains life of its sanguine force.

Yet Lefebvre does not exchange one ideology for another. In his critique of capitalism and Soviet communism, which does *not* become a new religion, he adds that to undo the collective state of alienation in which we find ourselves, we are obliged not simply to be "intensifying production" in the sense of manufacture, or "industrializing agricultures [...] building giant factories," but above all we must be thinking of "changing the State and then finishing once and for all with that monster, of all cold monsters the coldest" (1991a: 226). The aim ought to be to change quotidian reality, a given "state of things," in order to counter the effects of the State, which he takes to be the hydra or octopus whose tentacles reach everywhere and suck the life from all living matter. Lefebvre is especially clear in asserting that a revolution in everyday life involves far more than changing "lifestyles" that are the cloth of consumerist ideology.[3] Revealing everyday life in both its positive and negative aspects is a first step in a critique that aims at posing and resolving the difficult conditions of "life itself." A critical appreciation of Marx, not religion, can offer an effective, constructive, salubrious critique of life through its consciousness of a "new man," a figure akin to Nietzsche's *Übermensch* who, far from dominating and controlling the world, is the individual who invents it. The "world," Lefebvre reiterates," is man's future because man is the creator of the world" (1991a: 226–27).

Lefebvre's world soon changes and so also does his theory. In 1956, when writing a Foreword to the second edition of *Critique of Everyday Life*, the enthusiasm he shared regarding the advent of heightened affect and creativity is dampened. He cautions his readers about the pervasive impact of consumer technologies, the ubiquity of which cause him to emphasize the need to "adjust" his earlier writings, which had dealt with "the way in which everyday life lags behind what is technically possible" (1991a: 8). Drawing examples from *Elle* magazine's descriptions of newly equipped kitchens and Madame Express's prescription of must-haves for any woman (which Jean-Luc Godard's film, *Two or Three Things I know about her* [1966] would soon deploy), Lefebvre notes that the way in which "modern techniques have penetrated everyday life has thus introduced into this 'backward sector' the *uneven development* which characterizes every aspect of our era" (8). Technical advances are too often accompanied by a further degradation of everyday life for large numbers of human beings both in the city and in the country, in Paris and in France at large.

The displays of luxury that Lefebvre and millions of spectators witness in a flurry of mediocre contemporary films are shown, in his eyes, acquiring an almost fascinating character. The spectator is momentarily displaced into a not-so-everyday world where we are not only inured to our alienation but also led to enjoy it.[4] In the realm of cinema in the 1950s

3 Lefebvre criticizes "lifestyles" in *The Production of Space* (1991b: 57) in ways that readers today do well to recall. "Lifestyle" is a term coined by the media and cannot be distinguished from consumerism.

4 For Lefebvre the experience of cinema seems to antedate Jean-Louis Comolli's trenchant remarks, in direct derivation from Guy Debord's work on the society of spectacle, that sum up the state of film at the end of the first decade of the twenty-first century. "Perhaps the continuous flow of alienation becomes its own bliss, and perhaps spectacles, images and sounds first of all entrance us with the goal of having us *enjoy alienation* itself? Is spectacle content with serving as merchandise? And what if it were to become the supreme form of merchandise?" (2009: 9).

and 1960s, the medium is that which colonizes desire and fantasy, and as a result lived space gives way to a world fashioned by Technicolor images. Because the everyday is distinguished less and less from uneven development or else is obfuscated beneath screens of images directing collective fantasies and desires, critical and cultural analyses must be made to reclaim the register of experience—which indeed takes place in the continuum of space.

Urbanization of Space and Time

Lefebvre abruptly shifts his critical focus from the country to modernity, specifically to urbanization. The erasure of the demarcation between city and country that follows the rise of consumerism and technological development leads Lefebvre to write *The Urban Revolution* (1970; English trans. 2003). The critical take is again double. First, he retraces the history of the vanishing division between city and country that are distinguished by their respective forms of subjectivity and community. The city itself, which had its apogee between the sixteenth and the nineteenth centuries, when a balance held sway between politics and the market, is shown to be disappearing. Secondly, he brings out possibilities offered by what he calls the "urban revolution" that, relaying a failed Marxist revolution, signals the transformation of a former paradigm, not just the reform of an existing one (2003: 45).

The urban revolution is the fourth and penultimate stage in Lefebvre's periodization, which moves initially from an agricultural phase to a feudal condition and then to a world of industry. His concentration on urbanization gives way in 1974 to what is implied (presciently, it may be added) to be a fifth and final stage, the global production of space. Anticipating the advent of the world market, Lefebvre notes in 1970 the disappearance of the city both as a formal and a political entity.[5] The country had given way to urban development, and now the urban center belongs to a worldwide network of agglomerations of roughly identical character. Among his Marxian brethren Lefebvre is immediately criticized both for proclaiming prematurely the end of the industrial society and for a non-orthodox approach that sustains his vision.[6] In retrospect,

---

5 A comparison with the work of Lewis Mumford (1961 and 1970) would reveal similar approaches and conclusions.
6 A student of Lefebvre, Manuel Castells, in *La Question urbaine* (1972) [in English as *The Urban Question: A Marxist Approach* (1979)] accuses his teacher of romanticizing the urban phenomenon. Castells does not see the "urban" as a

almost four decades after his work was called into question, it can be said now that much of what Lefebvre called urbanization was linked to signs of impending globalization. In his writings of that moment he welcomes the demise of an industrial society that is synonymous with bourgeois capitalism and the domination of nature as well as people. He stakes his hopes on an "urban revolution" that will change existing concepts of space and time.

Seeking to loosen current social practices from the grip of industry, Lefebvre wants to orient "production" toward an emerging urban practice (or *praxis*) and to realize—rather than foreclose—its potential (2003: 76). He concedes that the urban revolution, the great product of modernity and consumer capitalism, nonetheless deprives people of existential ways of dwelling in the city. Economic pressures consign entire segments of the population to functionalist residences, often in the *banlieue*, the French suburbs, that were at the time the new living quarters for workers, the newly arrived *pieds-noirs* (French Algerians returning to France after Algeria's independence) and hundreds of immigrants from other ex-colonies or oppressive regimes. Yet, he maintains, the displacement can open up possibilities of invention when populations alter their *habitus* by grafting their practices on to—and thus emending—a number of shop-worn traditions. In the post-1968 era, at a time of worldwide protests against bourgeois industrial capitalism that had led to colonization and the alienation of students and workers, Lefebvre hopes for a different kind of unification that comes from the ground up. Doing away with the constraints imposed by the state and religion, urbanization *as it is lived* would further help to produce a new, emancipated, total human being. In the critical spaces this transition helps to open, Lefebvre now believes that humans can realize the possibility of reconnecting with their bodies and of becoming producers of space.

The urban zone rapidly becomes a global phenomenon that modifies relations of production without yet becoming a site of transformation. The critic's task is to forge concepts that will reveal the very terrain of the "urban," that is, of ongoing social practices in the process of formation (2003: 17). It is incumbent upon critics *and* artists to reveal the

---

viable scientific object. He also takes Lefebvre to task for abandoning a rigorous Marxist analysis. In *Social Justice and the City* (1973), David Harvey acknowledges his proximity to Lefebvre. Yet he rejects Lefebvre's assertions that the "urban" has supplanted the "industrial." For Harvey, industrial capitalism produces urbanization. Lefebvre's hypotheses of the urban and the production of space will become instrumental for writings on postmodernism by Fredric Jameson (1991) and Edward Soja (1989, 1996 and 2010).

degradation of the industrial paradigm and to find other ways of living everyday life in the urban milieu. How, Lefebvre asks in anticipation of the ideological and nascent ecological platforms of those who will become his spiritual children, is it possible to transform relations of production so as to build cities that will replace what was formerly called the "City"?[7] He predicts the emergence of a new order from within the grounding ambivalence that at the time is likely to inspire arguments at once for *and* against the street, for *and* against the monument, for *and* against urbanism. As in the cinema of the 1920s and 1930s, the *locus classicus* is the street, what had been the lived space in which the city itself took shape and which now meets its demise. Throughout France (and especially in Paris) the street had been the space of socialization but also of resistance and revolution. It was progressively lost when Haussmann redesigned its shape to prevent protests at the same time as it became cluttered with merchandise, inviting the pullulating growth of commodity-fetishism. It prevents any integral constitution of a subject or a group. Similarly, the monument, that which marks the official places of a city, becomes a monolith of repression that imposes spatial practices aligned with public pieties of religion. Yet the same monument opens to creative practices when the streets that lead away from it enable people to gather and create a new social space for themselves.

When discerned in its contradictions, Lefebvre claims, space can be unhinged from its former relations and changed into something productive. In 1970, a moment when state policy dictates that the cobblestones of the streets of Paris be covered with tar and asphalt in order to prevent the stoning of automobiles and armored police that students performed with fragments of pavement they lifted and threw at symbolic objects, no one knows what paradigms will emerge.[8] Earlier, industrial society had spelled the death of nature. In the industrial city, a second or built nature born of signs has replaced nature (2003: 25). "Natural spaces" were reinvented under the name of parks and gardens. When it is "simu-

---

7 The spiritual children are many and often are affiliated with Fredric Jameson's work on politics, literature and culture. Among others, we might name Richard Terdiman, *Discourse/Counter-discourse: The Theory and Practice of Symbolic Resistance in Nineteenth Century France* (1985); Kristin Ross, *The Emergence of Social Space: Rimbaud and the Paris Commune* (1988); Scott Durham, *Phantom Communities: The Simulacrum and the Limits of Postmodernism* (1998).

8 The slogan in 1968, *au dessous des pavés la plage* (below the stones the beach [or the bedding of sand on which they were placed]) translates the euphoria of the street and the doubt about what might be the landscape of the future. Lefebvre was clearly marked by the "May of 44 days," which saw the State and its bureaucracy come to a momentary halt.

lated," nature (and space) becomes *fictive*. Lacking the force of nature, the city-space of gardens and parks corresponds, Lefebvre concludes, to a degraded form of democracy. Yet, when it stops listening to the blather of abstract urbanist discourses that champion the "modern" and "modernism," the new urban society can again find creative and active forces within itself. Urban planners who continue to operate under the paradigms of the industrial age are content with imposing spatial effects on creative acts that occur solely in the intellect but never in desire or in the body. Homogenized and homogenizing, the industrial city did not facilitate creativity and invention (2003: 28). By contrast, within its own heritage an urban space emerges, a space that consists of many different communities in which contradictions and uneven development abound, but where possibilities for creative change nonetheless arise.

In one of his great signature historical flourishes, Lefebvre claims that the industrial city became the template for the homogenizing vision of bureaucrats, technocrats and advertisers. With the urban revolution, however, this period of homogenization is coming to an end. On the threshold of globalization, society becomes aware of its contradictions and takes on an urban form that allows the city and the community to be positioned in a larger and now more global context. Today the city, the country and the world are actively interdependent. The emerging city is constituted by another space-time and a topology distinct both from the agrarian cycles and from the homogeneous industrial periods. Each place exists only within a whole through the contrasts and oppositions that connect it to and distinguish it from others (2003: 37). Critics, he claims, might do well to look at new concepts such as isotopy, heterotopy and utopia.[9] After a period in which they were experienced ambivalently, places such as streets, paths, gardens and parks begin to exist in more differential relations to one another. An unforeseen "elsewhere," a virtual *non-place* that looks for a place of its own, has also to be accounted for.[10] In Lefebvre's eyes the utopian is not only what is abstract but also what is both virtual and real. Moreover, despite of planners' ongoing efforts to homogenize them, cities remain "differential." Lefebvre wants to "illuminate" all of urban society that extends into the past and into the future along this new plane of *difference*. In a more and more globalized world, he claims (perhaps uncritically) that his method of illumination is valid as much for Paris as for New York or Tokyo.

9 Lefebvre's allusion to heterotopia reminds the reader of Michel Foucault (1984).
10 Both Michel de Certeau and Marc Augé use the term "non-place" in slightly different ways. See Chapters 2 and 4.

Emphasizing the positive impact of force and desire over reason, Lefebvre argues that the "urban" is a complex field of tensions, a possible impossible. Collective blindness comes from the fact that many are content to see only things or objects according to their names and not the tensions and vectors that move through them. Urbanism continues to borrow objects and products, operations and technologies from the previous epoch of industrialization. In 1970 city-planners remain blinded and fixated upon a false clarity in retreat from an informed view of the complexity of life's actual conditions. The discontinuities between the industrial and the urban periods of development are smoothed over by officials who have the erroneous idea that humans are living as they had several hundred years ago, somewhere between the agricultural and the industrial societies. If this blindness toward the possibilities and demands of industry had not existed, would people have allowed it to "invade and colonize the world; to ravage nature and sow the planet with horror and ugliness through the course of a blood-soaked history" (1991b: 41)? Marx, Lefebvre flatly declares, wrongly believed that people could guide the process of industrialization.

Every regime has its own ways of alienating and dis-alienating its subjects or citizens. The feudal regime had its concentration of property which led to a demand for land. The industrial regime instituted the paternalism of the company, the family and the head of state. The hierarchies of this society were experienced as family and neighborhood relations. Exploitation appeared for what it was. The rise of industrialization in concert with the new relations of capitalist production revealed the characteristics of peasant and feudal society that were veiled within a turbid transparency for those who "lived" them without understanding them. Similarly, with a new intelligence and sensibility the urban milieu reveals the industrial counterpart, which now appears as a political and social hierarchy paired with refined forms of exploitation. During this vast process of transformation, space reveals itself to be the site and object of various strategies and struggles.

Urban practices, Lefebvre warns, cannot be determined by feeding data to computers. The machine thinks along binary lines and not in the existential complex of dialogue and open-ended dialectic that by their very nature never reach synthesis. Lefebvre makes a passionate plea: "Knowledge cannot be equated with skill or technique. It is theoretical, provisional, changeable, disputable" (1991b: 59). It is based on invention. Challenging technocrats or "specialists" who think that philosophy no longer has meaning, Lefebvre asserts that philosophers must provide a radical critique of all "finalisms" or of what he irreverently calls the obstacles of "economism, sociologism, and historicism—as well as of particularisms." He joins those who decry the fact that, since Hegel, philosophy has become institutionalized and is in the service of the state. It gives answers rather than asking questions. Intent on classifying and structuring needs through statistics and data, institutions in the service of the state close off *becomings* (1991b: 65). However, prior to any orientation toward a future, there exists, for Lefebvre, an impulse, an "élan, a desire, will, vital energy, drive" that, in its openness to becoming, also undoes the concept of linear, rational historical teleology (1991b: 65). A "*metaphilosophy*" will be able to address this critical situation productively and let a new language emerge. Since social, urban, economic *and* epistemological spaces cannot provide a platform for meaning, he concludes that space is not a norm, but "only a medium, environment and means, an instrument and intermediary" (1991b: 73). It never exists in itself but always refers to something else such as time. No absolute priority, condition or category of space prevails.

Spatial Practices

Four years later, in 1974, in *The Production of Space*, Lefebvre pushes his analyses of the urban arena even further. A generalized production of space, he now claims succinctly, has subsumed the urban revolution. Humans produce space and they, in turn, are produced by it. From the chiasm he derives his well-known conceptual triad that distinguishes between spatial practice, representations of space and representational spaces.[11] Representations of space are tied to relations of production and to an order that imposes these relations, hence to knowledge and signs. They are technocratic and rational. Representational spaces, however, embody complex symbolisms that are sometimes coded and sometimes not, linked to the clandestine and underground side of social life as well as to art. Space has to be considered with the intellect but also with the senses, that is, with the "total body" that is not alienated. Only then, Lefebvre asserts, pushing the moment of the hoped-for unification further into the future, do we become aware of the productive nature of conflict. This awareness of conflict will lead to the demise of official abstract space, which the state sets in place and corporate capitalism brings to

---

11 It can be said, in anticipation of Chapter 2, that *representations of space* are akin to Michel de Certeau's notion of *place* while *representational spaces* are synonymous with his concept of *space*. The relation of Lefebvre to Certeau seems complex and is in fact rooted in Situationism.

perfection. It will lead to the production of a space that is other or that is a matrix for heterogeneous communities of migrants and other displaced populations. Thanks to the potential energies of a variety of groups capable of diverting homogenized or industrial milieus to their own purposes, space might be restored to need *and* desire by means of differential systems and valorizations (1991b: 391).

In 1974 Lefebvre recognizes that space is even more divided or striated than he had previously argued. Western rationality is increasingly refined into new organizational forms, structural aspects of industry and modalities of total systematization. Here are located the forces that business, the state, the family, the established order and both corporate and constituted bodies deploy, it seems, in willy-nilly ways. In the opposite "camp" Lefebvre sees those who continually seek to appropriate space. They are comprised of traditional resisters, that is, various proponents of self-management or of workers' control of territorial and industrial entities, communities and communes, and what he calls "elite groups" (critics, theorists and artists) striving to change life and to transcend obsolescent political institutions and parties. The philosopher establishes an opposition between commerce, the state and intellectuals or artists that parallels another between need and desire, between things rational and irrational, technocratic and artistic.

Lefebvre continually warns his readers that abstract space—which can be taken as a tool of domination—is what the state deploys to eliminate vital differences. In 1974, as he moves along the parabola of a growing critique of classically Marxian concepts, he finds that Marx's theory of alienation now seems trivial. Considering the magnitude of the threats now facing human beings, the concept of liberal or "humanist" ideology is no longer an issue to be denounced. Failed urbanization results in the exclusion of differences from everyday life. A real theory of difference would open on to the unknown, that is, on to rhythms, on to the circulation of energy and the *life of the body*. Repetitions and differences would give rise to one another, harmonizing and disharmonizing in turn (Lefebvre 2004).

In the last pages of *The Production of Space* Lefebvre emphasizes repeatedly that theory always has to be adapted to a changing world. No one can escape the trial of space (*l'épreuve de l'espace*), which he also calls an *ordalie*, that is, something that forces you to react. Lefebvre makes it clear—though many of his followers (such as Edward Soja) persist in overlooking this point—that he is not writing specifically for geographers or urban planners. He is keen on developing a *metaphilosophy* that makes possible a critique of what exists and enables the emergence of other spaces. New ways of perceiving and conceiving are necessary to reinvent everyday life *and* the cities of tomorrow. In the process, the raw distinction between use- and exchange-value remains incontrovertible even when the world market dominates through the imposition of commodities and, as Lefebvre had already predicted, increasingly through the imperceptible flow of capital. Yet in a more and more technological era social space proceeds directly *from the body*, through repetition and difference, that is, through a form of rhythm. While arguing for a return to a *body in space* beyond philosophy, Lefebvre calls for the abolition of the arena of Western metaphysics from Descartes to Hegel that champions "state thought," and for the reintro-duction of a spatial reality that is continually reinvented.

To realize the potential of the period of transition in which our lives are lived he preaches that we must begin by distinguishing economic growth from social growth, power from knowledge, and abstract space from differential space. At a time when nature was known both for its largesse and for its cruelty, art was said to imitate nature. Today, nature has become a *second nature* less through art than through science. Any science that focuses only on analyzing data and on recognizing trends rather than on inventing the new is faulty (1991b: 410). Science has taken a direction that has yielded a plethora of things in space with phallic valence. Such a valence has also affected other disciplines. In history, emphasis on the male principle has led to warfare and violence, and in aesthetics to straight lines and right angles. Lefebvre wants to destroy phallic space by fomenting a "feminine revolution." Romanticizing women by placing them a priori on the side of the body and of enjoy-ment, he credits them with the power to end violence. He emphasizes anew the importance of the arts, especially of poetry and music.

In their transition from industrial to urban society humans live *between* a mode of production of things in space and the production of space where body and mind will once again be joined. Lefebvre is conscious of the importance of networks and of a change in scale that is happening with the onset of globalization. Differential space, he insists, has to be seen on a world scale. Modifying his earlier analyses, Lefebvre now states that, in a global world, the fabric of everyday life has become so threatened that a politics that would assure its permanence is also at risk of being lost. Lacking agency, human subjects remain unable to appropriate space or acquire the status of citizens. At the same time, far from being revolutionary or even improving the state of the world, poli-tics has become a hyper-specialized machine that is completely disconnected from social spaces.

Lefebvre seeks to create a society based on new modes of production in which social practices would be governed by different conceptual determinations. He sets these practices on the "road of the concrete," on the quest for a production of space that requires active intervention on the part of one and all. Only thus could a true *revolution of space* subsume the urban revolution and transform everyday life. He continues to hope that what is misunderstood today will be at the center of future thought and action so that a revolution of space will indeed lead to new modes of becoming. Critical of both bourgeois and what he calls Soviet-style capitalism, Lefebvre continues to envision social experimentation through collective ownership.[12]

From the post-war years to the mid-1970s, Lefebvre ceaselessly adapts his concept of space to an evolving situation in France. He shows that, with impending globalization, space becomes a player in the politics of the redistribution of nature, of new demographic pressures and of policies (absent and present) concerning worldwide pollution. He ends his *Production of Space* by claiming that on the horizon,

> at the furthest edge of the possible, it is a matter of producing the space of the human species—the collective (generic) work of the species—on the model of what used to be called "art": indeed, it is still so called, but [this] art no longer has any meaning at the level of an "object" isolated by and for the individual… (1991b: 422)

Such an art would be collectively produced.

Lefebvre envisions the future creation (or production) of a "planet-wide space as the social foundation of a transformed everyday life open to myriad possibilities—such is the dawn beginning to break on the far horizon" (1991b: 422). It is, he declares, the same dawn as glimpsed by the utopians who inspired Marx and Engels. Similarly, by means of his dreams, fictions and desires, Lefebvre wants to offer *real* suggestions toward the production of a total body in space. To avoid defining a trend, Lefebvre speaks "advisedly" of an orientation. He is concerned with what, with hesitation, "might be called 'a sense': an organ that perceives, a direction that may be conceived, and a directly lived movement

---

12 Lefebvre criticizes Soviet revisionism of the "capitalist process of accumulation" while praising the "'Chinese road' [that] testifies to a real concern to draw the people and space in its entirety into the process of building a different society" (1991b: 421). He claims that the Chinese focus not only on wealth and economic growth but also on the development and enrichment of social relationships. This method, he declares, implies the "production in space, the production of a space ever more effectively appropriated" (1991b: 421). Such a process would minimize uneven development. The passages praising Mao's Cultural Revolution give today's reader pause.

progressing towards the horizon", that is, "with nothing that even remotely resembles a system" (1991b: 423).

Lefebvre quand même

Despite their anthropocentrism and their failure to heed the fact that the human species has done untold damage to the ecosphere, Lefebvre's words have a nostalgically soothing effect. Published almost forty years ago, and roughly thirty years after the liberation of France from the yoke of Nazi occupation, they reflect the climate in which they were written. In the midst of urbanization Lefebvre argues for recognition of desire, for creativity and for the body that he hopes will live in (and thus create) space prior to and beyond the symbolic contract that language imposes.[13] His utopian body will breathe in the atmosphere of the everyday according to rhythms of difference and repetition in such a way as to overcome the divisions imposed by capitalism. In *The Urban Revolution* and even more so in the work of 1974, Lefebvre sees possibilities for such a space that would be under collective stewardship. It would have an element of spontaneity, desire and conflict, and it would entail negotiation and participation among the most diverse human parties. It would transform everyday life on a planetary scale and lead to new possibilities.

In his preface to a new French edition of *The Production of Space* published in 1985, Lefebvre becomes stridently critical of the utopian aspects of his earlier writings, including *The Production of Space*, and deplores the fact that he did not offer an effective critique of growing urban ghetto spaces.[14] He also admits that his project for a "new space" was not sufficiently outlined. However, he reiterates the "usefulness" (or use-value?) of his writings because they focus on discerning the actors of production and oppositions such as public and private, exchange and utility, state and intimate family, frontality and spontaneity, space and time. His preface is meant to pre-empt the double accusation of creating

13 Michel de Certeau, who is indebted to Lefebvre, especially in *The Practice of Everyday Life* (1984), develops a different concept of the body, closer to language and psychoanalysis. See Chapter 2.
14 In *Space, Difference, Everyday Life: Reading Henri Lefebvre* (2008), Kanishka Goonewardena et al. periodize the reading of Lefebvre to identify a "turn" from *spatial* to *urban*. They make a compelling and convincing argument for reading the philosopher in today's context of urban problems and minorities. Urban problems, of course, can never be studied separately from questions of space or habitability.

a *utopia* (a fictional construction born of 1968) and an *atopia* (in the aftermath, elimination of a concrete space in favor of a social void that silences protest and its echoes).

What are we to make of the philosopher's ceaseless musing and unending desire to create habitable spaces? Lefebvre becomes utopian because his bodily cognizance of the state of the environment was either romanticized or because his concept of *production* was based on blind faith in industrial growth. It was the residue of an inherited doctrine in which the environment was not an issue, or at least was far from the complexity it now has. In his argument for the body and for use rather than exchange, he addresses tangentially the precarious conditions in which we now live. Though he writes about the return to space as related to scarcity and pollution, he is more focused on the parceling of nature as real estate and the fact that it has received more critical attention than the city. In "The Right to the City," published in French in 1968 (1996: 157–59), Lefebvre criticizes the focus on nature as a means of escaping from urban life and points rightly to a much-overlooked, increasing effect of segregation in cities. At the time of its disappearance, people suddenly want to buy a right to nature.[15] Instead, everyone should be given the political right to the city, a *droit de cité*. Yet these cities, he omits to add, have to be sustainable. To be energized, the lived body is in need of clean air and water. In his efforts to create habitable spaces, Lefebvre sometimes anticipates but also skirts ecological dilemmas that have since become far more compelling.

At once an ideologue and a visionary, prolix, heated by the fire of contradiction and revision, a writer lacking the elegance of Aristotelian concision, Lefebvre nonetheless marshals powerful arguments for the everyday world, the world in which an ecology of space is made possible that is not a passive *habitus*. Lefebvre sees himself writing in an increasingly "global" world that is also one of rampant scarcity and pollution, a world in which space is the symptom of its dilemmas and, no less, the site of their solution. His is a plea for life outside of the perimeters of abstract space. The cry for a non-alienated body and for a new sense of everyday life, endowed with another sense of space/time coordinates, may now seem charmingly romantic. Yet it whets a desire to create other spaces in the places we inhabit. Lefebvre's labors are most effective when they displace the "old" or existential apprehension of alienation in the ambient world into the regime of the "new" or of the accelerated homog-

15 This is what Marc Augé studies in many of his texts, especially in *Domaines et châteaux*. See Chapter 4.

enization of existence—which he clearly foresees even before the global reach of capital has made known its effects and consequences. As a foil and complement to Lefebvre, the contours of Michel de Certeau's creation of new spaces now need to be addressed.

2

Michel de Certeau: Anthropological Spaces

Space is a practiced place.
Certeau, *The Practice of Everyday Life*

Space is existential, existence is spatial.
Certeau, *The Practice of Everyday Life*

At the heart of Lefebvre's writings on cities it is the urban planner who serves the state to shape a collective *habitus*. Dwellers in metropolitan centers, he notes time and again, have the task of using their milieus creatively, often at odds with the designs imposed upon them. The words are astonishingly similar to those of Michel de Certeau in his writings on everyday life. Lefebvre emerges from Marxist philosophy and history while Certeau counts, as François Dosse has shown (2002), as an *inclassable*, a writer who approaches space even more eclectically and from a variety of angles that include the history of religion, anthropology, linguistics, city planning, psychoanalysis and sociology. Certeau writes a cultural anthropology that discerns the unconscious religious tenor of everyday life. His discipline is one which mixes late medieval theology with Maurice Merleau-Ponty's aesthetic and existential philosophy, from which he borrows the distinction between *anthropological* or symbolic and *geometric* or administrative spaces. When all is said and done both Lefebvre and Certeau deal with ways of living and of being in the world that, when juxtaposed, yield remarkable similarities and differences.

Everyday Practice in a Bureaucratic State

Geometric sites, Certeau argues, are those that a state and a disciplinary regime impose upon their subjects.[1] They exploit architecture, urban

1 *The Practice of Everyday Life* has a variegated history. First compiled for a popular and left-leaning publisher (Union générale d'éditions, '10/18', 1980), it was then translated into English by Steven Rendall (1984). The French original, the first panel of a diptych (of which volume II deals concretely with the everyday), has a different title, *L'Invention du quotidien 1: Arts de faire* [The Invention of Everyday Life 1: Arts of Doing]. The essay was revised, re-edited and brilliantly

29

planning and available technologies to project their mental and physical design on to members of the *polis*. The state, he reasons, locates and confines its subjects by means of technological controls that bear resemblance to what Michel Foucault had defined as the apparatus of the disciplinary society or that which imposes a preconceived order upon the citizen. Technologies in the service of power establish "geometric" spaces of abstraction of the kind Lefebvre had analyzed. Certeau mirrors Lefebvre in seeing in the post-1968 era both the apogee and the failure of a regime seeking to imprint an order on its subjects, on the nation and on the world. For a brief moment, he is even hopeful that May 1968 might enable citizens to capture speech—though he too is intensely aware of a world whose *lingua franca* belongs to consumer capitalism.[2]

The mystical tradition informing Certeau's work (his doctoral thesis was on Jean-Joseph Surin) is of a tenor that locates in the physical world deeply embedded signs of creation and presence that are far from those that capitalism puts up for sale. Written for colloquia, sponsored by governmental inquiries, or aimed at monthlies such as *Le Monde diplomatique*, Certeau's political essays, going hand-in-hand with *The Practice of Everyday Life*, are products of circumstance. Reflections on pressing questions of the day, they resemble erudite sketches drawn *in medias res*. They introduce the past into the present in order to open on to the latter a perspective that the former makes clear, effecting change in the best of all worlds to foster the democratization of the world for egalitarian ends.

A prime question he addresses in the 1960s and 1970s deals with the impact of technologies and consumerism on French citizens. Continuing what his fieldwork in Latin America had shown him, Certeau argues that in France too, against all expectations, a diverse popular culture maintains and reinvents itself within the matrix of a controlling regime. The practices of popular culture become a form of secret and covert resistance to the repressive or homogenizing forces under the sway of rapid

---

introduced by Luce Giard in 1990 (Editions Gallimard/Folio, a popular format), four years after the author's untimely death at the age of 62.

2 Certeau adumbrates the notion of capture. He observed that the stumbling block for protesting groups was speech itself: lacking an idiolect of negotiation, whatever demands they made could only be fashioned in the language of the state. If even they were crafted to address the state, their words would be couched in the vocabulary and syntax of the oppressor, and thus would be ripe for defeat because no available words could convey their needs. In much of the first half of *The Capture of Speech*, anticipating the conclusions of Gayatri Spivak's celebrated study on the speech of the subaltern, he notes how gesture, performance and theater took the place of speech.

modernization and technologization. The everyday becomes the site where passages are opened, and where space and language are the raw materials of collective and anonymous creativity. The ordinary person, far from simply complying with the dictates of order, invents his or her own ecological spaces, which remain opaque to the administrative or military forces of order.

Touching upon yet another dilemma of the post-68 period, in his political writings (and to a lesser degree in *The Practice of Everyday Life*) Certeau expands the frame of his reflections to ask what changes the nation-state undergoes with the nascent European Union and the presence of an increasing number of cultures and their practices within its space. He asks: in a postcolonial and globalizing world how does the nation rethink borders and border crossings? How does the state receive and host foreigners? How does it deal with other cultures? How, within the state, can cultures exist in a plural condition? What happens not only to outer but also to newly erected inner borders? An acute awareness of technology and human ecology informs Certeau's views, which, far from simply embracing a global theory of culture that would be synonymous with a happy "family of man," show how theoretical pronouncements are in fact circumscribed both historically and geographically.[3]

To define what he means by the anthropological space with which these practices are affiliated Certeau focuses on *l'homme ordinaire*, the ordinary man whose genealogy reaches back to Georg Simmel and Sigmund Freud. He deals with creativity in what he considers a prevailing condition of spatial compression marking the character of disciplinary societies.[4] Centralized and bureaucratic regimes, observes Certeau, seem to unravel under the pressure of popular resistance. An exemplary, albeit brief, collapse was witnessed with the counter-cultures of the 1960s, but

3 Certeau writes in the preface to the English translation of *The Practice of Everyday Life* (1984: ix): "In translation, analyses that an author would fain believe universal are traced back to nothing more than the expression of local or—as it almost begins to seem—exotic experience. And yet in highlighting that which is specifically French in the daily practices that are the basis and the object of this study, publication in English only reinforces my thesis. For what I really wish to work out is a science of singularity; that is to say, a science of the relationship that links everyday pursuits to particular circumstances. And only in the local network of labor and recreation can one grasp how, within a grid of socio-economic constraints, these pursuits unfailingly establish relational tactics (a struggle for life), artistic creations (an aesthetic) and autonomous initiatives (an ethic)."

4 "The ordinary man" has been much criticized. Marc Augé, in *Non-Places* (1995), finds it reductionist since it homogenizes. However, Certeau sees it close to *le petit peuple* who, while exploited by the elite, continue to oppose various tactics of resistance.

the latter nonetheless belonged to a newly emerging consumer society. On the one hand, the so-called counter-cultures "captured" speech that before the events of May they had been unable to formulate, while on the other their demands could not be met within the growing global economic sphere. When students and workers joined hands to engineer a national strike a rift was opened in the disciplinary apparatus of the state.[5] When the force of speech diminished, all the signs indicated that they had not been seeking a better world in which to live, a world less scarred by uneven economic development.

The task of the disciplinary bourgeois society to which the counter-cultures belonged was felt to be the elimination of diversity or archaic traditions in order to optimize the "legibility" and smooth functioning of the social milieu. May 1968 did not reduce the number of subjects conditioned and controlled for maximal production of signs and commodities. How, asked Certeau in September 1968, in such an environment can the citizen-subject manage to live and resist being "subjected" by the order in which he or she happens to be? How can the individual become a subject with agency? Or, how can the subaltern speak when no language is available for negotiation? An answer is found where people invent "tricks" or "ruses" that enable them to bypass the mechanisms of controlling systems. When faced with official dictates, with what Gilles Deleuze called "order-words" imposed in the name of technological and administrative efficiency, or when required to follow pre-traced itineraries, the ordinary person finds a means of inventing his or her own paths in quasi-unconscious everyday tactics that work contingently, locally and otherwise in the midst of the effects of official strategies. These tactics consist in invention, in other words (etymologically), in *happening upon* or *choosing*. To the static notion of place, the locus of the proper where administrative organization prevails (the police station, the schoolroom, the office), Certeau opposes dynamic spaces (the sidewalk, the kitchen, the subway) that owe their pertinent traits to choices and actions.

Special emphasis is placed on the narratives that their users, the anonymous "people," at the same time ceaselessly invent. The lessons of May 1968 showed that the "lived" always goes through language. Drawing on J. L. Austin's theory of the speech-act (synchronously and in unspoken accord with Jacques Derrida's critique of that theory in the final chapter

---

5 Highmore (2002: 145–73) offers a rich and comprehensive view of Certeau's dialogue with Foucault and its resemblance to British movements of the 1930s. Many of his points are redrawn in the paragraphs above.

of *Margins of Philosophy*), Certeau adds a further spatial twist through Freudian and Lacanian psychoanalysis, the "human science" in which concentrated attention is paid to the advent of language following the child's separation from the mother's body. In an implicitly psychoanalytical reading of the events of 1968 he noted how a generation born after the Second World War separated itself "into" the space of the nation and its apparatus. The generation felt itself broken away from the maternal order of the state and at odds with its paternal or dictatorial character. It is here that the awareness of ambient constraint was met by invention—that is, the creation, negotiation and practice of space.

City-Spaces

Certeau turns first to the compression and the transformation of urban areas that he considers to be administrative milieus *par excellence*. In France and in Europe in the late 1960s cities changed radically when new modes of development turned France into a site of economic "revolution."[6] Focus is placed first on the masses—students, workers and immigrants—who find themselves swept out of the nation in which they were born and yet told to retain it as their affiliation and identity. To raise his argument to a higher level of abstraction and to specify how the "state" controls its subjects, Certeau looks toward the established theoretical claim of the supremacy of the visual in Western culture. To see is to conquer and control; it is also (etymologically) to theorize, to bring into view and to be enabled to judge by discerning different objects in the greater depth of a visual field.[7] Power invents the fiction of seeing and of making the city legible in the idioms it imposes.

Here Certeau applies his own "tactical" fiction of everyday space, a groundbreaking study of "polemology," the science of war, in the urban milieu. The city planner imposes a model of life that appears efficient,

6 The term aludes to John Ardagh's classic sociological account of the 1960s, *The New French Revolution* (1968). Ardagh studied the impact of the reorganization of Paris, its plan for development in the direction of Normandy along the shores of the Seine, and *remembrement*, the agrarian reform that turned small plots of land separated by hedgerows into fields that new tractors could easily manage.

7 The preface to *The Writing of History* (1988: ix) revisits the "mirror stage" or stage separation into the modern world through a close reading of Jan van der Straet's copperplate image of Amerigo Vespucci, having just reached the shores of the new world, "discovering" the attractive nude, rising to greet him from a hammock, whom he will control visually in his field of view and aurally when he names her in echo of his own Christian name.

simple and transparent, a model that inhabitants traverse *contrarily* within its templates. Every official order of control yields a deviant or delinquent response. No sooner is a strategy imposed than it meets with counter-tactics. The practices of everyday life are foreign to and thus escape the grasp of the city planner, engineer or architect. Tracing maps and plotting itineraries of their own that for tactical reasons are invisible, inhabitants craft their own spatial fictions and, more often than not, invent ecological solutions to the dilemmas before them. They make much from little and indeed create hybrid forms of behavior. Their practices are, in Certeau's words, "networks of mobile, intersecting writings and manifold stories."[8] The fragments of these trajectories, impossible to inventory or classify, can never be totalized. They continuously alter existing spaces so as to foment "minuscule revolutions."[9] They are, for Certeau, remains of another, migrational and metaphorical city. This migratory force of sorts that continuously evades the city-state order does not really escape it. Rather, within its boundaries, it finds means of creative invention and subversion; thus, in accord with his concurrent work on mystical behavior, Certeau concludes that the ordinary person becomes the "wanderer," the "migrant" or Chaplinesque pilgrim who slips through the network of sanctioned modes of control.[10]

The state seeks to totalize, that is, to make visible and legible its site and situation. We may recall that for Henri Lefebvre totality meant not synthesis but the recovery of a lost plenitude, the reconciliation of the mental and physical dimensions of the lived and living body. For Certeau totality of this kind has a negative inflection. Unified, seamless and faultless, it is opposed to the fragment, the milieu or the topography in which spatial stories will take place. These partial and ever-anonymous stories are never rid of the geography of official places, nor do they dismantle the relation of power that they impose: yet they shift and change received notions of what constitutes a place and skitter around the area of the

8 (1984: 93). In his writings, Certeau assembles pieces from different contexts and situations in order not to convey their points "in the fiction of a metalanguage unifying the whole work" (1992: xxvii), and to be sure that the sum is a "fragmented discourse" from whose fissures and openings further invention can issue. His is a politics of form and style.

9 The term is borrowed from Jean Ricardou's *Révolutions minuscules* (1971), which used arduously formalistic prose to counter the grandiose political pretensions of the Marxists of 1968 who, it now seems sanctimoniously, promised the advent of greater revolutions. Certeau is an adept at modest but effective "minuscular" practices.

10 The mystical figures—Surin, Labadie and others—whom Certeau studies in *La Fable mystique* (1982) tend all to be travelers and nomads whose destinations are not as exact as those of pilgrims.

nation-state in which they are exchanged. The modern European city was founded on the concept of a "proper space," that is, of a clean plan with which its administrations expunged what it called "physical and mental pollution." However, like the repressed, space "returns" as a critical concept in what Certeau first sees as everyday practices and especially the results of May 1968. Hindsight tells us that the return was prompted by the advent of globalization, which causes the city to break away from the nation-state. As a result, the city functions both as a place of appropriation *and* transformation.

Style, Certeau declares, is a fundamental element of identity and difference, at once of spatial invention and of a way of being in the world and positing an *ethos*. For the city-dweller, his or her *practices*, from walking to talking and cooking, are a "stylistics" of everyday life. Urban pedestrians are poets whose footsteps mark a measure and a beat of their own. By choosing to ambulate where their feet lead them they turn the city-places into *other spaces*.[11] They also change these places. Certeau devises a rhetoric of walking whose intensities cannot simply be reduced to abstract information or easily categorized to what Bruno Latour will criticize as the zoom effect or double click of the mouse.[12]

Through these diverse spatial ecologies a faith in the world can be restored. Certeau praises what he calls collective singularities that generate a "long poem of walking" into which wanderers insinuate other itineraries. Created are other geographies that undo the official rhetoric of power (1984: 105). At stake for the cultural theorist is the making *habitable* of a place by introducing a space of play or by crafting an opening that is both mental *and* physical. While a more static *place* consists of a configuration of positions, *space* exists only as vectors of direction, velocities and variables of time. "Space occurs as the effect produced by the

11 I use *other spaces* to establish a contrast with Michel Foucault's pathfinding and contested article of that title, in which he coined the concept of a heterotopia where different practices could take place without conflict or hierarchies among them (1984). He located them on boats floating outside of the continental masses. David Harvey (2000) takes Foucault to task by suggesting that the heterotopia resembles a touristic cruise.

12 Certeau's poetical politics have been criticized because of their echoes of Heidegger and for their bracketing of various modes of mechanized individual and public forms of transportation. In "Railway Navigation and Incarceration" (1984: 111–14) he argues that travel in rapid trains strips users of spatial agency by transforming them into simple passengers. An existential fear of confinement, much like what a reader of Sartre encounters, is found here. On Sartre and immobility, see Hollier (1982). Hollier notes that the existential hero is one who walks in the ambient world and not one whose ambulation is enabled by prosthetic means. Sartre's heroes do not own drivers' licences.

operations that orient it, situate it but also temporalize it," and thus it can be formulated that "space is a practiced place" (1984: 117).

To mobilize his argument Certeau expands further on Merleau-Ponty's distinction between geometrical and anthropological space. Merleau-Ponty, he claims, distinguishes a univocal experience from an outside, for which "space is existential and existence is spatial" (1984: 117). Hence an appeal to the *Phenomenology of Perception*:

> This experience is a relation to the world; in dreams and in perception, and because it probably precedes their differentiation, it expresses "the same essential structure of our being as a being situated in relationship to a milieu"—being situated by a desire, indissociable from a "direction of existence" and implanted in the space of a landscape. From this point of view, there are as many spaces as there are distinct spatial experiences. The perspective is determined by a phenomenology of existing in the world. (1984: 117–18)

Emphasis is placed here on space and time as they are experienced in an individual's consciousness of a landscape in which he or she happens to be. The invention of space belongs in part to a world of dreams and the unconscious that is in play with active experience. Where space—or language—is lost the field of possible experience shrinks and limits human possibility. The existential practitioner uses stories and narratives to relocate the places where they are told. He or she inserts space into place.

National Places

Yet stories can also help consolidate place when they serve as foundational narratives for a nation-state. To contextualize further the actualization of space through everyday practices, Certeau adds the problem of national spaces that pervades France as a result of the Second World War. Economic development in the post-war years, the constitution of the European Union and decolonization complicate the existential model. Many histories of nation-building, as Benedict Anderson (1983) and others have shown, construct illusions of national identity. These illusions are fabricated commodities, signs deployed to make belonging to a nation-state appear either as a given (for those born within its boundaries) or something that can be earned (by those who seek to become citizens). However, in his typically phenomenological drift, Certeau reminds his readers that national spaces exist only in their articulation with others, and that just as there exist conflicts of nations there also exist competing illusions of appurtenance. Identity becomes a psychomachia, a battlefield of mind and body. Bridging these realities and illusions, which is of utmost importance, requires encouragement. Nations and regions are by definition spaces created through such bridgings (1984: 126).

Working on re-articulating the limits of geography and subjectivity, Certeau concludes that people and nations establish borders in performative actions when they say who and what is authorized to cross them. Borders have to be turned into crossings and rivers into bridges. Borders and bridges oppose *and* meld together. While official instruments delineate and striate space, stories straddle mental and physical realms, much like metaphorical bridges. And as geometric places are haunted by anthropological spaces, so also is the city as concept by metaphor, and the colonizing map of the nation by a figuration that, for the sake of its authority, it had previously elided: law and order always summon their inverse in "delinquency" and "illegality." At the same time as codes regulate and serve to enforce the laws of place, something else moves along the interstices of the codes and opens or creates a space that undoes and displaces their order. Such is what happens, in turn, when popular narratives are reintroduced into the official foundational story of the nation-state: when taken literally, the story, foremost in spoken form, becomes the very principle of mental and physical mobility that flows within and across the channels of official discourse. Much like popular hagiographies, stories are introduced into foundational narratives of the nation by anonymous groups to imagine the idea of places in creative ways.[13] It remains to be asked: what then happens when foreigners arrive in France and introduce *their* narratives into that of the French nation-state?

From Spatial Invention to Ethnic Encounters

In the disciplinary society described in *The Practice of the Everyday Life* "ordinary" people insinuate spatial stories and practices into the dominant order in their midst. They actualize in people's daily lives what official stories had sought to do to cement the nation into the minds of its citizens. After 1968, however, the French nation-state loses its universalizing as well as its foundational narratives. What had been taught according to the Napoleonic codes was antiquated or no longer appli-

13 Official hagiography is one thing, and its popular rewriting is something else. *The Writing of History* opts for the latter. For Certeau, "popular ignorance" is folklore (*avant la lettre*) on to which the stories of Christian saints have been grafted (1988: 276).

cable to the current world. The history of the Gallo-Roman era that gave way to the Merovingians and then to the Carolingians and then to the Capetians, and so on, could only carry meaning for a public needing practical formation. Decolonization and changing demography explain why. With the onset of economic globalization, migrants arrived in France and Europe more often than not from ex-colonies in numbers that threatened the official fiction of the homogeneous nation-state.

In the mid-1980s Certeau was called upon by the Organization for Economic Cooperation and Development to study immigration and its impact in France and in Europe. What in "Ethnic Economies" (1997a: 141–74) he calls the "shock" of encounters, both a physical collision and a mental reaction, takes place at the borders but even more so inside societies that in their urban situation are rapidly becoming composite and heteroclite. The nation-state that once identified with what had been constructed to be the space of *one* culture, based on the principles of the Revolution, becomes pluralized. Borders that defined the nation now criss-cross the areas they formerly surrounded. Certeau shows how immigration produces an eclecticism that commercial, industrial or media technology has been quick to appropriate. In the 1980s the reigning society is no longer under bureaucratic management but rather a function of strategies, which control the effects of diversity. As a result ethnic "heteronomies" are leveled when they submit to the general codes of individualized diffusion through marketing (1997a: 160). When they are pitched to a consuming public, cultural differences that assure the invention of space are subsumed in the universalism of a dominant culture via procedures leading to *assimilation*. When a universalism eradicates cultural plurality the risk of confrontation ensues. Under the guise of "hybridity" consumer culture produces a "hybrid monism" that does away with the conflicts between *real* differences.

However, migrations continue to alter the dominant character of national and cultural spaces by subverting them from within. In what Certeau sees as encounters (and occasional confrontations) between cultures, adaptation is imposed more violently on immigrant or minority groups whose cultural practices, while being detached from their original setting, acquire an unforeseen importance in their new environment (1997a: 161). Two traits are distinguished. The first, active, of belonging, figures in a cultural practice that is often spatial while the second, passive, is based on the fortunes of cultural memory. Certeau situates both in the transformation of belonging to a community and a homogeneous space. In such a context, in France from the 1980s onward, conflictual relationships between hosts and immigrants produced an increasing obsession with "national" space (1984: 162). The French state supports and even encourages the resulting ethnocentrism because it finds itself in the process of losing power to transnational companies that call into question the ideologies of community and nation.

Certeau notes that while a market economy, in addition to capitalizing on cultural differences, simultaneously erases the imagined geography of national borders and the narratives that supported them, at the same time the state encourages a new focus on nationality and thus increasingly on territoriality. While it is said that the French think along the lines of given truths (France is a "melting pot" that welcomes populations from its ex-colonies, etc.), Certeau declares caustically that the idea is more a product for export than a domestic practice. Since 1789 the French have been experts in the export of universalistic ideas and the dream of the coexistence of different groups. In practice, they belie the theory. Today, the existence of any social group results from conflict. Groups are no longer autonomous but built upon this very conflict.

Such conflicts happened in the 1980s, argues Certeau, between France and the Maghreb, especially Algeria. The situation can be generalized to include immigrants from any number of other places. The ideological, historical or mythical representation that a host or immigrant group confers upon itself at a certain moment also pertains to the struggles it is engaged in. Any group is de facto in constant transformation, and even more so now with the acceleration in transportation and global communication. Representations of the nation are designed to express a timeless essence about a community born of an exceptional history when, in fact, any family is always riddled with contradictions. To conceal this fact French officials turn representations into what Certeau calls "monuments of identity," what Lefebvre had called representations of space. Inter-ethnic confrontations, however, precipitate crises of traditional representation. With migrations, stability of place—including territory and language—disappears both for the host country and for migrant populations. The former can no longer simply identify with official representations of the latter while internal struggles arise all the more readily as traditional symbolic structures and their inherent hierarchies are no longer respected (1997a: 164–65). As a result, not only the groups themselves, but the very nation-state where migration takes place begin to mutate. The state becomes progressively more heterogeneous and, *in fine*, different forms of minoritarian clusters are born, varying according to the registers they use.

Certeau opposes conditions to operations. Actions and specific "styles of being in the world" are linked to cultural and spatial practices, which include first and foremost ways of speaking. The language a group speaks is less important than the *use* it makes of it, that is, its *performance*, which appropriates the dominant language and opens new spaces. According to the model of *The Practice of Everyday Life*, accented idiolects—such as *verlan*, the popular youth slang of the *banlieue*—introduce play in a dominant field.[14] They lead to inventiveness within the field of power by which a community continues to influence linguistic behavior. Young people subvert and reappropriate the dominant language and infiltrate musical as well as literary culture. They create mental and physical territories. In Certallian terms, much like the "wanderers" (*Wandersmänner*) of early modern Europe who populate his *Fable mystique* (1982), immigrants invent new ecological spaces by introducing *other* inflections into official discourses so as to dislocate the orders that direct them.

Despite these inventions, the ways a community shares in living in a space are often maintained while the objective conditions of the habitat shift and change. They allow the new environment to be appropriated while transforming it. If, Certeau argues, immigrant practices can survive the move and if they are more characteristic than the spaces in which, for a time, they find themselves, it follows that in their displacement these practices should be granted a right and a means to exert themselves in everyday life (1997a: 169). A group uses specific activities to invent its history and participate in new ways of territorial construction rather than be alienated by identifying with its places of origin. In other words *bridging* no longer extends between nations but between cultures that transform spaces and the practices both of the immigrant group and of the host group within the state itself. The very principle of French universalism has to be rethought since the nation is now made up of multiple communities defined by their ever-changing cultural and spatial practices. The French can no longer simply defend "their" space from the "errors" and "barbarisms" of foreigners (1997a: 170).[15]

To account for and indeed to foster a transformation of the city and

---

14 The problem of the relation between a "dominant" national language and its subversion through the introduction of tensions and play is the subject of much *banlieue* literature and film by Mehdi Charef, Farida Belghoul, Azouz Begag, Amara Lakhous, Rabah Ameur-Zaïmeche, François Begaudeau and Laurent Cantet, to mention only a few.

15 We note a tension between Certeau as anthropologist and as sociologist. Anthropology allowed him to move toward a political sociology. When he was writing his political essays cultural demands were tied to a slackening of the economy due to a transformation of the nation-state in the matrix of flexible capital. The reader senses that he is keenly aware of changes taking place with the advent of the consumer economy.

the nation-state, Certeau focuses on the necessity not only of traveling mentally and physically but also of translating. The danger consists in believing in continuity between cultures and their practices—including language—where there is none. From anthropology to linguistics, in disciplines that Certeau sees born of the "West," wrongly assumed continuities and homologies are deployed to impose various arrays of practices on others. These disciplines gloss over the heteronomies that exist between different types of linguistic practices, which lead to the construction of what soon after Bruno Latour will aptly call different worlds.[16] French pedagogy often mistakenly assumes that language, obeying different rules, is a single reality in all societies. Humans live in different realities—or worlds—with different concepts of space and time. In "The Long March of the Indians" Certeau had shown how language functions for the Chiapas and what the consequences are for their construction of reality.[17] In "Ethnic Economies" he claims again that spoken languages are different social practices in the Maghreb or in France.

> Languages are distinguished by norms but also by ways of functioning that are qualitatively foreign to one another. For one group, they are the spiritual edifice of a founding reality. For another, they objectify a network of compatibilities and exchanges among individuals. In still another society, they participate in the bodily staging of acts. These differences enable one to perceive the errors of the innovations of ways of speaking the marks traced in a given language such as French by a practice that originates in a geographic and psychic elsewhere. Each time they are signatures of different uses and gestures relative to other ways of doing things and of acting. (1997a: 169–70)

While some codes such as music, fashion or food, Certeau argues, move easily between cultures, others pertaining to symbolic registers do not. Language corresponds only to one regime of symbolic practices. The organization of time and space, of law, marriage and family, heritage, penal codes, medicine, cuisine and bodily care are all essential places of a society affected less *through* objects, tools or concepts than by ways of appropriating, using or thinking across and through them. The results of compromises and adaptations, cultural practices are conventions, often hardly coherent, that are never registered as such. When immigrants implant practices they produce aporias by making use of what a new milieu considers to be defunct.[18] Like many of Certeau's "ordinary prac-

---

16 Latour (2002). See Chapter 7.
17 Michel de Certeau, "The Long March of the Indians," *Heterologies* (1986).
18 This is shown in the film by the Dardennes brothers, *La promesse* (*The Promise*, 1996). The young African immigrant woman from Burkina Faso uses space in a way that, for Igor, the young man who cares for her after her husband dies, is both archaic but, unexpectedly, also productive of openings.

titioners" of everyday life, immigrants may no longer know the meaning of the words or the references in the quotations they use to guide their daily lives. However, the latter linger on; they even induce and inspire invention that keeps an ethnic alterity alive.

Ongoing cultural and linguistic translation and negotiation are crucial for the avoidance of violent conflict. Certeau convincingly shows that commercial enterprise often exploits cultural codes and opens them to marketable cultural exchanges. Yet among immigrants, resistance to assimilation by the host country is found in certain symbolic practices that include ways of perceiving, occupying and creating space in the host country. The latter create differences that can lead to hostile encounters but also to productive conflicts, which make visible the homogenizing fiction of the former nation-state.[19]

Immigrant Spaces: Certeau with Azouz Begag

Certeau's anthropology of mixed and indeterminate space in the immigrant experience has echoes in a growing body of literature and cultural theory. His work has served as a template both for the construction and the reception of a "heteronomic" body of practical and politically effective writings that can no longer simply be categorized under the rubric of "francophonie."[20] Azouz Begag nuances the immigrant experience which he sees as strongly related to the experience of space and time. The son of Algerian immigrants, Begag, who grew up in a shanty town near Lyons, writes at a time when the numbers of immigrants have increased so much that the infrastructure of the nation-state is beginning to collapse. Novelist, sociologist and former delegate minister for equal opportunities, Begag, writing from the point of view of the immigrant community, concludes that those from North Africa cannot be reduced to a simple common denominator. At the same time, when they depart from Algeria or other places for France their immigrant frame of mind is active. They do not leave for the unknown. They seek an established Algerian network that is already in place, yet the displacement itself

19 Etienne Balibar reaches similar conclusions in his interview with Catherine David (1995). See Chapter 8.

20 The category of "francophonie" is under scrutiny even in France where it was recently dismissed in a manifesto for a "littérature-monde" or world literature by 44 writers from all over the globe: "Pour une 'littérature-monde' en français. Le manifeste de quarante quatre écrivains en faveur d'une langue française qui serait libérée de son pacte exclusif avec la nation" (Barbery et al. 2007).

causes existential anxiety which in turn primes the desire to develop a micro-community within the greater matrix.

In order to help its outsiders become acclimatized to the social and urban fabric in the host country, resident citizens *must* empathetically consider the immigrants' representations of space and time (Begag 1989). Begag cautions against reductive generalization by stressing the importance both of individual or group experience and of geography and history. If we borrow our notion of time from phenomenology, he asks, can we define a group simply as "immigrant"? Individuals, based on their personal past and projects for the future, define their position at the present moment and in view of the circumstances that bear impact on their lives. Individuals and the group, quickly influenced by the host community, accept some changes based on the need for cultural compromise; others may be resisted, even rejected. In the latter case, conflict with the host country ensues. The ecological space that the immigrant community carves out and occupies changes over time.

To look for differences beyond the stereotypes they purvey, Begag underscores the significance of temporal and spatial coordinates. Putting aside the question of how immigrant spaces are transformed under the impact of globalization, he focuses on historical changes that determine what immigrants do to live in a now-global economy. Work requires them to be more readily drawn to cities where the sexes will benefit differently. It is often women who emancipate themselves when they are obliged to change their cultural practices. Such changes may occur where cultural constraints are eroded, but especially where poverty influences representations of space or position in society. In *Quartiers sensibles* (Sensitive Neighborhoods, 1994), Begag argues that with the appearance of cable television, immigrants withdraw and acquire a false feeling of security.[21] Instead of entering the political fight for what he too calls existential space, they give themselves over to nostalgia by watching television programs from home. Their imagined mobility hides the frustration of their immobility. In order not to confront the hostility of the housing complex, the neighborhood and French society, immigrants withdraw into the fictional spaces of televised images often broadcast from their home country.

Critical of the government and its urban planners, Begag argues that

---

21 In the film *Salut Cousin* (1996), Merzak Allouache treats this theme humorously. Alilo, having come to Paris for the purpose of "bizness," visits his aunt and uncle who, from their HLM, capture Algerian programs with their cable television. Alilo remarks that in Algeria, by contrast, everyone watches French channels.

the great open spaces, the linear and regular construction in the name of a modernist vision of physical and mental hygiene, have "planted boredom" among those who must live in their midst. The flat terrain was the ideal for the *barres*, the long, rectangular buildings of the housing estates. This vision, according to the Charter of Athens which dealt with habitability, was supposed to liberate its inhabitants from the "weight of history" and of "the street" that, in Begag, takes on a negative connotation.[22] Eighty percent of all French people live in a city. He claims that they identify with a neighborhood, a center, a modern day agora of sorts, and have available sizable open spaces that are the very condition for mental health. The inhabitants of the *banlieue*, the suburbs, must also have such ecological spaces to free themselves truly from the weight of colonial and immigrant history and from the street. The children of the *banlieues* dream of wind and open spaces. They also dream of water, which inspires him to appeal to a passage from Gaston Bachelard's *Water and Dreams*, in which the then-Jungian analyst declared that, because of its blue color, the sea appeals to our unconscious and to our childhood. Begag concludes that, even if only metaphorically, water and the sea would help to irrigate thoughts in the *quartiers en difficulté*, the neighborhoods in distress (1994: 181). He associates artificial waterways with the possibility of walking, or browsing about (*flâner*) without an immediate goal. Between what he calls "rouiller" (literally, to rust or rot) and "s'arracher" (to tear oneself away from one's setting), the *flâneur* creates a third or other space. While the French inner city offers itself to strollers, similar ambulation is impossible in the *banlieue*. Begag concludes that it is an "ecological imperative" to reinstate this function that is essential to city life in all the sensitive neighborhoods. He quotes from François Maspéro's *Roissy Express: A Journey into the Suburbs* (1994), which replaces clichéd and racist reductions with a spatial narrative: "There is no citizenship without *flânerie*, without time to listen to others, to meditate oneself and get out of the logic of war and power to enter into one of [human] exchange."

Also inspired by Merleau-Ponty, Begag joins with Lefebvre and Certeau in combating the loss of existential spaces and the eradication of a sense of dwelling. To invent ecological spaces, to make "dwelling" possible, a housing complex has to be irrigated, infused with "water"

---

22 *Quartiers sensibles* (1994: 178–79, my translation). For the Charter of Athens on "dwelling," see *Alternances urbaines* (Centre Georges Pompidou/CCI, 1979), cited by Begag. The original Charter of 1943 that, under the impact of Le Corbusier, focused on the "functional city," was revised in 2003. Emphasis is put on the quality of life, that is, on habitability and sustainability.

that makes possible flow and *flânerie* (1994: 182–83). Immigrants are too often excluded from walking and talking, that is, from turning place into space and from creating anthropological spaces in the hyper-functional residences to which the host nation-state assigns them. Noting that the dysfunctional aspect of these neighborhoods mirrors that of an entire society, Begag argues that the media uses information to eradicate the plurality of collective memory. The *banlieues* suffer from marketing and the deformations wrought by televised images that often discourage the creation of existential spaces. "While journalistic logic continually imposes its urgency, everyday life in sensitive neighborhoods continues and founds its life stories" (1994: 184).[23] Begag has the Certallian gift of emphasizing existence as a spatial phenomenon and so reaffirms the drive to life of ordinary people as opposed to what he sees as the death-drive of the media. He finds a spiritual ecology and a spacing in the rhythm of reading as opposed to the consumption of images.

Creations of Space

Space, for Certeau and Begag alike, is less produced (as it is for Lefebvre) than created through dynamic movement and practice, first, among ordinary people who reinvent the everyday to "make" the city from heteroclite ways of living and, secondly, from the encounter between immigrants and natives. Begag's world is one of spatial encounters between what Certeau calls host and immigrant cultures that result in cultural pluralities complicating and transforming the official spaces of the nation-state and the city. The France that would be the "nation-state" is transformed under the force of migrations that are the result of decolonization but also of global capitalism.

On the heels of Begag, we can say that if water is to be the universal solvent of the dreams and realities of the immigrant experience, it is vital that it be free-flowing and both plentiful and potable. It is here that the anthropological spaces that Certeau theorized find renewed political virtue. Thirty years have passed since he developed his concepts of the "spatial story" and the "practice of everyday life." In that time these concepts have been amply criticized, to be sure, and often with good

---

23 This is shown in the film by Jean-Patrick Lebel, *Notes pour Débussy, Lettre ouverte à Jean-Luc Godard* (1988). Lebel revisits the same housing complex shown in Godard's *Two or Three Things I Know About Her* (1966) and rather than imposing his own view, makes the inhabitants tell their own stories about the invention of everyday life in a difficult setting.

reason.[24] Yet the sense of opening or of becoming that went with the concepts, as Begag shows, has not flagged. In the time since *Practice* and the application of its underlying politics, the world has witnessed considerable further shrinkage and meltdown. It would appear that what Certeau proposed, and what Begag confirmed and exceeded, attests to the right to an everyday existence and ecological spaces that is increasingly denied to populations moving in the global flow. Yet theirs are practices that leave "light footprints" on the places where they go, and theirs are recipes for an art of living modestly and generously in a world in need of these very qualities. Their virtues become especially salient when they are juxtaposed to Jean Baudrillard's reflections on contemporary space, the topic of the chapter to follow.

---

24 Nigel Thrift (2002) argues that existential humanism permeates Certeau's idea of the spatial story. He takes Certeau to task for omitting technologies. Thrift does not really touch on the spatial story in the context of immigrant experience.

3

Jean Baudrillard: Media Spaces

Mastery of space now leads to control in space.
Baudrillard, *The System of Objects*

Humans are distributed spatially, that is, by economics.
Baudrillard, *The System of Objects*

America has to be thought in terms of space and not of an existential territory.
Baudrillard, "L'Amérique et la pensée de l'espace"

"Cover the Earth": like the red liquid that drips over our globe in Sherwin-Williams' emblem advertising its brand of house paint, it can be said that a globalizing consumer culture covers the northern hemisphere and extends on to the sea and land below the Equator. The famous logo is a fitting allegory for the state of the world that theorists in the line of Lefebvre and Certeau in the post-war years, anticipating globalization, had called the effect of the bourgeois and the impact of the disciplinary society. In Chapter 2 I suggested that familial and ethnic networks lose their character when transnational economies redefine them. At a microlevel, argued Certeau, stories and myths that had been vital to everyday life and ecological spaces are now compressed into slogans and advertisements for the ends of economic development. We have seen more directly that his writings deal with ruses and resistances to what he and Lefebvre perceived to be the controls that the state imposes on its citizens through technology and consumerist ideology. Using psychoanalysis, in which the language of the unconscious plays a determining role in human activities, Certeau focuses on questions of existence in relation to place. Writing at the threshold of globalization, he is less interested in a sociology of space than in discerning how everyday practices implicitly subvert urban administration and how migrations are now transforming the shape and complexion of the nation-state.

Along this line of inquiry, Certeau's writings on space and place bear useful comparison with those of Jean Baudrillard. Baudrillard is fascinated by the same fascination that drives consumer-based media. Bearing a Marxian signature from his early writings up to his death in 2006, he

47

argues that new forms of capital, increasingly equated with transnational circulation of money and signs, eradicate popular resistance. "Workers of the world, forget about your chains, you need only switch your channels." He analyzes the mechanisms of control that are put in place while simultaneously focusing on a consumer world that, first, operates according to a model of feedback and cybernetics and, secondly, has an economic analogue in the differentials of "input" and "output." He dismisses operations that seek to "save" the everyday. What Baudrillard calls the "retro-movement" that held sway in the 1960s is now sensed to have been hopelessly utopian and futile (1991: 156). The implicit historical vector runs thus: by way of progress in communication and the media, the new regime that America set in place after the Second World War becomes "radical" in the 1960s and even more so in the four decades that follow. In France, it gradually transforms the disciplinary society and the secular ideals inherited from the Third Republic into a system of regulation and control. Functional systems of operation "unidimensionalize" (in the verb Herbert Marcuse had coined to advance a critique of capitalism) the field of human experience.[1] Financial flows that move across national borders weaken the administrative state; technology and the media enable the emergence of a new, more transnational order of supple but pervasive control. Baudrillard inserts his analyses at these levels where residual existential relations with the world are shown to be archaic. Those who are in power (the "power elite" of the era of C. Wright Mills) target existential relations for elimination or oblivion.

From the 1960s, the story goes, the bourgeois disciplinary society and the symbolic networks upon which it was based are eroded. The trend toward a functionalism, first identified in France under the impact of the Marshall Plan as an "Americanization" of the country, soon extends all over the world under the guise of a non-localizable system. The hypotheses require Baudrillard (like Lefebvre) to periodize capitalism. In the wake of structuralism in the post-war years a spatiality of speculation intervenes, a view of space plotted according to capital investment. Classical and industrial periods stand behind the 1960s, at which moment they give way to a new phase controlled, according to Baudrillard, by the "code" or a structural treatment of the economy. To these phases correspond three types of laws of value: the natural, the commercial and the structural (1983: 83). The cultural theorist notes in

---

1   When Marcuse taught at the University of California-San Diego in the early 1970s he met Michel de Certeau, a visiting scholar, who wrote a brilliant critical assessment of the man and his works in the context of 1968, *Culture in the Plural* (1997b: 91–100, especially 94).

the process the gradual unmooring of objects from their referents, in other words (as had been the case for Lefebvre) of signs from the objects they signify, and the supplanting of objects' original use-value by their exchange-value.

Setting semiotic theory into the mix of economics, Baudrillard radicalizes ideas held among Saussurean linguists about the arbitrary or motivated aspect of the sign. In capitalism everything goes: the sign is arbitrary, but for the end of profit it must be made to be motivated in every way possible. The relation of words to things is without prior cause outside of imposed convention. Abstract value is accorded to signs, which supersede what had been equated with things or even commodities. Baudrillard too develops the theory with emphasis on the visual and the image. He calls simulation the moment in history when images no longer feign or dissimulate—now, they merely simulate. With the transition from analog to digital technology, images no longer stand for a reality outside of themselves. Some of these transformations may free Western subjects and their colonized counterparts in the rest of the world from the fixed and assigned places they occupied in the disciplinary regime that went with the industrial era, an era whose ideology depended on the representation of a pre-existing world. However, they are soon caught in another, more virulently "coded" order made possible by cybernetic systems and the media that carry other hierarchies.

The new and dominant capitalist system that focuses on efficiency and smooth functioning in search of greater profits seeks to do away with cultural resistances at both personal and collective levels. The present system no longer works according to the rules of a symbolic exchange but primarily via feedback. In this new phase of capitalism, concepts too lose their metaphoric status, that is, they become bereft of their existential and, at a deeper level, theological "origin"—exactly what in the history of religion Certeau had seen present in all things. The result is that concepts, especially that of power, have been entirely transformed. One of the productive consequences of this transformation is that the so-called "real" of former times (what in life cannot be reduced to a sign and thus is vital to it) is now seen as a fiction belonging to the realm of discourse of another age.

From Object to System

Baudrillard observes that, beginning with the impact of post-war consumerism and commodity fetishism, new forms of exchange progressively alter subjectivities and reorganize private and public, national and even transnational spaces. In 1967, the date of the French publication of *The System of Objects*, he scans the interior of an apartment to analyze the transformation of bourgeois space in this new era. Created in the nineteenth century as a site of protection from a rapidly changing outside world, the interior is filled with objects whose symbolic meaning confirms the order that made the place possible.[2] The furniture itself is less telling than its spatial arrangement—a bedroom, a dining area with a table here and a sideboard there adjacent to the kitchen, and so on— which conveys a faithful image of the familial *and* social structures of a period. An intended spatial unity, he claims, carries the legacy of a moral unity (1996: 17). Objects personify human relations while humans who move amidst them have little autonomy. Objects comport a "density" and guarantee an official order, marking the very boundary of the house by which an interiority is assured. They are also spatial incarnations of emotional bonds and the permanence of a familial group. This type of furniture confirms the values of the middle class, which echo the persistence of family structures that enjoyed a certain immortality until, in Baudrillard's words inspired by new technology, a "new generation" displaced them. Now they are only objects of nostalgia for what is charmingly "old" (with emphasis placed on the redounding effect of inverted commas). The antiquarian furniture that embodied the official character of a given political group continues to sell. Today it often appeals to lower classes who are still living according to a familial order that no longer has currency, while a new elite is looking for another.[3] It has also begun selling again to more upscale customers as a means of stylishly recapturing symbolic values that have disappeared (1996: 16).

As objects change so also does the individual's relation to family and society. With the loss of the symbolic and its corresponding bourgeois obsession, interiority, persons are now free to turn toward the outside and invent a space of their own. Liberated from their symbolic functions, new objects lose the illusion of permanence granted through their weight and density. They suddenly become light, they fold, pull out and free

2 Walter Benjamin, "Paris, Capital of the Nineteenth Century" (1999: 14–26) is a canonical point of reference. Noteworthy is Rimbaud's sonnet, "Le buffet," which envisages a piece of furniture as a museum of relics of times past (Leuwers 1984: 54).

3 In Wim Wenders' film *Wings of Desire* (1987), two angels, Damien and Cassiel, living in eternity, are supervising human activies. Damien, played by Bruno Ganz, decides to leave immortality and join the mortals on earth. He walks down the street in Certallian fashion and pauses to make fun of a window display of just such a bourgeois interior.

themselves from attachments to a (symbolic) place. They point to a new concept of space all the while that the latter, compressed and expensive, is more and more at a premium. Because of demographic pressure, scarcity of space motivates changes that force inhabitants to adapt in a functionalizing urban environment. Places are no longer re-elaborated from a moral point of view and as a result more traditional spatial practices become very much endangered. When social relations were based on transcendent or fixed values, there existed a clear demarcation between inside and outside, private and public. Traditional space, Baudrillard concludes, bears a psychological sign of such immanence. People are assigned to the place a symbolic order governs. With no moral value, functional places are simply integrated in a structural system of value.

Within the symbolic house—in French aptly named *immobilier*, suggesting immobility—objects too "move" with difficulty. They embody permanence. By contrast, the now-ephemeral object is destined, as Walter Benjamin had shown in his essays on nineteenth-century Paris, to be replaced when it goes out of style. The "dwelling place" thus loses its internal organization and coherence. Though many critics note an equivalence between the loss of dwelling and that of existential space, Baudrillard makes clear that gains are apparent whenever individuals are no longer defined by their family and society or through their objects and places. Turned toward exteriority, people are free to invent space. The new social mobility (or at least its illusion) is accompanied by mobility in furniture that allows people to organize their space more freely. This freedom, he concludes, produces greater flexibility in social relationships. Yet the liberation is only partial since humans still depend on the object whose function alone has changed. When the new furniture with which we live is "liberated from ritual and ceremonial," we cease being practitioners of times past (even if we collect antiques). In France in the 1960s marketers and manufacturers fashion "things" that still bear traces of the old order while they are designed for the new functionalism of the serial object.

Consumerism and the serialization of objects cause substance to give way to an interplay of functions. At stake is no longer the "secret" of a unique relation but the "differential moves in a game" (1996: 21). The erasure of a radical distinction between inside and outside is accompanied by changes in interpersonal and social structures. Lacking inner "soul," objects lose the symbolic presence they had held in earlier phases of capitalism. Walls open up so that, according to what Baudrillard calls the "buzzword" of the day, "everything communicates" or is "connected" with everything else.[4] Objects no longer "correspond" to each other, they "communicate." Space is implied to play "freely" between them.

The freedom, however, that comes with the availability and ease of the ephemeral use-value in objects does not inspire resistance on the part of the "users," practitioners, à la Certeau, who invent openings and passages for ends of their own. No longer assigned to a place, Baudrillard's users simply manipulate objects as part of a combinatory system outside of which no action is possible. This order guarantees a dubious freedom of voluntary servitude under the dictates of media and advertising. By asking consumers to create a livable, organized space, a new elite also confers another hierarchy upon them. Interiority, which has been noted as a sacred part of bourgeois ideology, is replaced by the illusion of a more mobile exteriority. Organizational skills and effective means of problem-solving co-opt the opening of ecological spaces and the opening or fraying of passages that had been felt in their psychoanalytical and existential sense. Space, Baudrillard claims, is not so much "invented" or "created" as "mobilized" as a *response* to (and not a correspondence with) pre-given sets of conditions. Against Certeau, he declares that it is no longer figural but functional. The novel idea of "personalization" that advertisers promote conceals the functionalist ethos that "motivates" their conventions of character.

The impact is felt all over, especially in everyday life in which existence becomes functional. New constraints appear, many of which are due to the scarcity of space, while others are ciphered on the price tags attached to the objects that force people to adapt to mental and physical inflation. With this functional turn, time-held symbolic investments begin to vanish. Baudrillard writes: "When nature was the original substance, objects were seen as vessels and receptacles. Humans were bound symbolically, that is, viscerally to their objects" (1996: 28). The world of computation, by contrast, is an abstraction crafted, produced and manipulated. Today's readers will be amused to learn that for the critic this model functions only at what he calls a highly technical level that, in 1967, he equates with the tape recorder and the car. Baudrillard implies that the era of the *promeneur*, Certeau's practitioner of the spatial story, has been replaced by that of the drivers of cars who pilot their way to and from shopping malls. On this issue Baudrillard is categorical: any

---

4   In Jacques Tati's film *Mon oncle* (1958) Madame Arpel, a fifties housewife, while showing off her ultramodern suburban house to her friends, exclaims, "tout communique." All objects communicate or "are connected" to one another. The irony is that there is precisely no human communication in the new, ultramodern but aseptic environment. On this passage, see also Ross (1995: 105).

attempt to recover earlier cultural and spatial practices is in vain. Everyday life is still governed by some traditional forms of praxis even though they are no longer of importance in a changed political and social order. Though an object may still have such value for some people in France or elsewhere, this status is no longer valid in today's world-space. Objects with symbolic value are now relegated to museums. They are all part of a system in which no product, no matter where it is on the globe, can escape the formal logic of a commodity or of a sign.

The shift from a symbolic tradition to a functional system informs many literary texts and films of the 1960s and 70s which share much with Baudrillard's vision. Their conceptual basis could well be that of *The System of Objects*. They are often situated in urban milieus, from Georges Perec's *Choses, Un récit des années soixante* (1965) to Jacques Tati's films, *Mon oncle* (1958) and, even more so, *Playtime* (1967). *Choses* deals with a young petit-bourgeois couple whose dreams the media have fashioned and who thus have limited ambitions. The major protagonists, Jérôme and Sylvie, two market researchers, are really signs more than they are personages. In a narrative that is almost entirely in the conditional tense (they never *do* what they *would* do) fashion and signs determine their movement more than any visceral or existential desire of their own. Tati's films likewise show the progressive transformation of France by which a "symbolic bourgeois order" falls under the tide of American consumerism and technology. In *Mon oncle*, the existentially backward ways of Mr. Hulot and his neighbors who live in a traditional neighborhood are contrasted to those of a family of newly rich living in a gentrified zone in an ultramodern house built on the ruins of the old, where practiced space is replaced by functional ways of living. Putting the popular neighborhoods on the side of the more backward spaces associated with the everyday that he equates, at the same time, with a surplus of enjoyment, Tati, like the early Baudrillard, introduces class conflict into the smooth and seamless regime of post-war middle-class life.

Tati does this even more so in *Playtime*, in which people, especially American tourists, find themselves shuttled about in a functionalist universe. Iconic city views of the Eiffel Tower or Sacré Coeur are seen only as reflections in the glass doors and windows of the ultramodern buildings of sets reminiscent of La Défense.[5] Scenes that include a flower

---

5 Baudrillard, in "L'Amérique ou la pensée de l'espace" (1991: 159), comes to a different conclusion when he writes that in order to downplay the modern functionalism of La Défense, French architects and city planners built a small arch in order to reintegrate the neighborhood into the domain of history.

vendor in the street (perhaps an avatar of George Méliès?) are resurrected as artifacts of sorts for tourists who think they have found the "real Paris." Referential reality has been suspended. People watch television in their living rooms while from the street and through screen-like windows passers-by watch them as if they were in a movie. Movements are controlled; only fleeting tactics enable people to escape momentarily an encroaching system of control. Even cars are caught in traffic. They circle endlessly around a rotary as if on a merry-go-round, suggesting that a system's ideal of efficient circulation has collapsed into congestion and immobility.

Myths find themselves supplanted by functional mythologies born of technics, one of which is that of a false progress.[6] We need to challenge, Baudrillard urges his readers, the assumption that rationality of ends and means governs the technological project and its sphere of production. Technological society, which thrives on the myth of "progress," is said to crush the moral backwardness of humans. Moral stagnation, however, transfigures technological progress insofar as the system of production is absolved of responsibility. The supposed "moral" contradiction always hides the true social contradiction. From a Marxian angle Baudrillard criticizes the media that proclaim the benefits of technological society while masking the existential fact that the new mode of production works only for technical progress and not for the ends of fostering social relations. The media propagate the myth of a happy convergence between technological production and consumption that masks all political and economic counter-purposes. An entire civilization, Baudrillard declares dramatically, comes to a halt (1996: 126–27).

Far from being a technophobe at the time of *The System of Objects*, Baudrillard declares that technology could help to produce—though it fails to—a more meaningful world of "communication." The car is once again exemplary because, as an object that could bring humans closer together, it is what separates them, first by its price tag and then, if cost issues are overcome, by the promise of isolation in which the driver is placed. Rather than focusing on recovery of the everyday, on the invention of ecological spaces and on popular resistance to the state, Baudrillard shoulders the responsibility of uncovering the lies perpetuated by a new dominant order. Helped by the media, a new elite constructs other hierarchies that operate according to the principles of a new functionalism that is still dressed in the antique language of an earlier social order.

6 Roland Barthes wrote on contemporary myths in *Mythologies* (1957), a collection of occasional articles that book-ends *The System of Objects*.

The Loss of Geopolitics

Ten years later, when writing *Simulations* (1977), Baudrillard theorizes that the loss of referents and the intensification of cybernetics and feedback systems further compress time and eradicate space on a worldwide scale. He claims that humans now live in a structural order where exchange-value entirely subsumes use-value. His earlier findings are reiterated to emphasize more directly that cybernetics belongs to a global flow of communication and information. With the loss of referentiality and the gain of simulation existential territories and geopolitics have disappeared. Everything transmogrifies into pure abstraction. It is this state of things that Baudrillard calls the "desert of the real," the arid climate of a new imperialism that causes the real to coincide with simulation. He quickly appropriates recent scientific language to claim that simulation is "nuclear and genetic." No longer either metaphysical or mimetic, it is neither discursive nor speculative and neither a mirror of being nor of appearances. The "real" is now produced from matrices and memory-banks.[7]

It is a Lacanian truism to say that without the real there can be no imaginary, and that without its resistance to language any sense of dwelling is gone. When nothing is hidden and all is exposed, the unknown is known. Places are no longer magical, welcoming, threatening or even haunted. Existential territories are eradicated. We—Baudrillard never specifies to whom the first-person plural refers—are left with combinatory models in a *hyperspace* without atmosphere (1983: 2). Yet the liquidation of places and points of reference occurs simultaneously with the resurrection of a system of signs that are more "ductile" and "material" than those that had carried meaning. This new system lends itself to optimal efficiency through all systems of equivalence. Simulation is a substitution of the real by a kind of media hyperspace that extends all over the globe (1983: 4). A space of exteriority, regulated by the flow and exchange of capital, causes human subjects, regardless of where they are located, to belong to a world comprised of the exchange of signs and images.

Lacking the fiction of the "real" at the basis of the bourgeois regime, people turn to nostalgia or to myths of origins that freeze the past in museological or mummified time. Certeau had earlier noted how the

---

7 Baudrillard's expression "the desert of the real" (1983: 4) is cited out of context (but with astounding economic success) in the film *The Matrix* (1999) by Andy and Lana Wachowski. Spoken by Morpheus (Laurence Fishburn), his words are adopted to refer to a world of destruction.

media appropriate cultural differences, but Baudrillard now goes one step further to declare that when ethnology dies, people invent an anti-ethnology that revives differences everywhere. In a consumerist world-space, such a revival can only be *artificial* insofar as simulation yields a seamless, functionalist, data-driven universe that eradicates both history and geography or time and space. The fact that much of humanity does not—yet—live in ways outlined by the critic does not invalidate his argument. To illustrate his theory (long before the construction of EuroDisney, a proof of his premonitions) Baudrillard studies Disneyland and the city of Los Angeles, two places that had become the point of attraction for a whole generation of French theorists—Jean-François Lyotard, Michel de Certeau, Louis Marin, Jacques Derrida among them—in the 1970s. In Los Angeles and Orange County he finds a functional universe devoid of any stubbornly remaining furnishings (or Rimbaud's "vieilles vieilleries") from the old world. Disneyland is a "model" of entangled orders of simulation in which gadgets and objects simulate "warmth" and "affection" by causing those who walk through its space to forget the solitude of a world bereft of anthropological relations. They conceal the omnipresence of a structural law of value. Applied to Disneyland, Baudrillard's *Fiction of the Real* attests to the loss of reality and space in Orange County, the area in southern California whose name indicates that groves of trees bearing citrus fruit have given way to shopping malls. A sense of place is given in the very history that the toponym brings forward, where otherwise it is taken (at least by those who cannot read the past into the present) to be a self-given "non-place."[8]

The task of the critic, as it had been for Lefebvre, nonetheless entails unveiling the unsettling truth to those deceived by conglomerations of a power elite. The critic has to reveal how the media make people believe that by regenerating public morality they regenerate capitalism. Based on competition and profit the latter dissimulates its contradictions by continually invoking a strengthening of morality. Yet the very immorality of capital cannot be dealt with in a system of moral and economic equivalence that has been the axiom of leftist thought from the Enlightenment to communism and beyond. Capital, Baudrillard declares, is never linked to a contract, including the social contract. Simulation unhinges linear continuity or dialectical process, which would be a vital critical element. The "precession of simulacra," Baudrillard argues, is the parade of the

8 Marc Augé reaches a similar conclusion: "[E]mpirically measurable and analyzable non-places whose definition is primarily economic has already overtaken the thought of politicians, who spend more and more effort wondering where they are going only because they are less and less sure where they are" (1995: 115).

illusory that defines simulation.[9] "Facts" now arise at the very intersection of models, which leads to the dramatic conclusion that all existential spaces or territories are illusory.

In 1977, nonetheless, simulation and more ecological—or what Baudrillard calls archaic—spaces are still mixed. Under capital the intention is to liquidate these spheres and, with them, the so-called traditional cultures that had sustained them. Simulation, Baudrillard cautions, is more dangerous than the archaic violence and transgression out of which it emerges. It is suggested that law and order, which had been understood in terms of reality, can actually be simulated. Parody—what for Certeau had been an invention or a counterpractice, a *logique de perruque*— cancels the very difference on which the law is based. When only models exist, the real (which assures the presence of existential territory) and parody (an existential relation to a territory otherwise deprived of existential options) are diminished. Mixed spaces vanish when capitalism, which initially fostered the reality principle, becomes the first to undermine it by deterrence, abstraction, disconnection and *deterritorialization*. Through the imposition of the equivalence of signs in all areas of life every possible value is undermined. As images are sold, disconnected from the real things they once signified, so also houses, places, culture and politics are deterritorialized along with the human body.[10] The bourgeois *subject*, based on interiority, gives way to a *citizen* who under capitalism turns entirely toward the outside and the market.[11] The law of capital becomes the radical law of equivalence. Baudrillard concludes that the production of the real in the digital age is hysteria, which is the very domain of the media and politics.[12]

Baudrillard's vision of recent history informs an implicit concept of space. The shift toward the law of supply and demand signals the end of the panopticon, Foucault's emblem of a disciplinary system based on the controlling power of the gaze, which had prevailed at the beginning of the nineteenth century.[13] The era of the disciplinary society is followed

9   In a critique of Baudrillard, Latour writes that there are no models, only processions. See Chapter 7.

10 This is the topic of Simone de Beauvoir's novel, *Les belles images* (1966).

11 Jean-Luc Nancy (1993) argues that the monarchic subject gives way to the democratic citizen who, however, easily comes under the spell of capitalism. To avoid being subjected entirely to the law of the market, the "subject" must reside in the citizen. See also Etienne Balibar's concept of the *citizen-subject* in Chapter 8.

12 Paul Virilio echoes Baudrillard in the *City of Panic* (2005), taken up in Chapter 5 below.

13 In *Forget Foucault* (2007), Baudrillard is unjustly critical of Foucault whom he accuses of focusing on an "older regime." Yet Foucault makes it quite clear that he is writing about a regime that humans are about to leave.

by that of the *test*, the regime in which manipulation becomes an order that informs what would seem to be stable signs of truth and falsehood.[14] By the mid-1970s (when Foucault elaborated the idea) the panoptic order comes to an end. Baudrillard, discovering television, writes (deliriously, it seems) that now "you are the model, the social, news, the event. TV watches you." Gone are the subject, the focal point, the center and the periphery. "We cannot isolate the effects of a media that is viral, endemic and has a chronic present" (1977: 54). TV dissolves into life, life into TV. Thus the media have a sort of "genetic code" that controls the mutation of every real thing into a *hyperreal* simulacrum. Perspective and everything it had enabled from the time of the early modern period up to now is relegated to the past. Elided is any gap or space between reality and meaning, which is so important for the construction of existential territories.

By quickly inventing new critical concepts borrowed from recent research on DNA and the atom, Baudrillard envisions this brave new world. TV, he writes, functions according to a genetic model of DNA, to nuclear contractions and to the retraction of a schema that, until now, has maintained at least a minimal distance between two poles (1977: 56). This distance has now disappeared and with it earlier paradigms of time and space. Quick to adapt results obtained in laboratory conditions to explain a messy world-space that always introduces stubborn resistances, Baudrillard concludes that any gap has vanished into a genetic coding process. The indeterminacy is not one of molecular randomness but the abolition of any relation. Order, signal, impulse: a message *is* information rewritten in terms of inscription, vector and decoding, a dimension of which we know nothing.[15] It is no longer even a dimension when it is defined in terms of Einsteinian relativity by the absorption of distinct poles of space and time. Nothing separates one pole from the other, he concludes emphatically, or the initial from the terminal. We can only say what no longer is. In the regime of simulation causality and meaning implode. In disciplines such as biology and psychology, Baudrillard chants with seemingly cynical glee, wherever distinctions between poles cannot be maintained simulation takes over. The latter is not based on passivity but on a non-distinction between active and passive.

Only a simulacrum of conflicts is left in a data-driven world intent on leaving nothing to chance. As Baudrillard put it, purged of every threat

14 Gilles Deleuze reaches a similar conclusion in "Postscript on the Societies of Control" (1995: 177–82).
15 1977: 56–57. It is again Latour who refutes Baudrillard when he argues that there is no information, only a cascade of transformations (see Chapter 7).

to the senses, the entire universe becomes understood in terms of norms and deviations. It becomes "aseptic" and thrives on technical perfection. Formerly, the law brought with it an aura of transgression (the formulation of a law inviting its infraction or violation). Violence in the symbolic sphere tapped the imaginary. Every finality, every contradiction or complexity that had once been common to the lived experience of social relations is now examined by the truth of statistics. With satellites, even the earth shrivels and becomes excentric, hyperreal and insignificant. This system, whose users are obsessed with deterrence and norms, eliminates all personal, social or national resistances, including primal, pre-capitalistic structures that had been found in the "mixed" space of which Baudrillard had formerly written.

American Space and French Territories

Focusing on unveiling the "tendency" of the world, Baudrillard is not an evil genius without any pangs of ambivalence about what he observes and seems to promote. Highly critical of the capitalist reinvention of space in globalization that he equates with the Americanization of France and of the world, he is also, as we can read in one of his books with the same title, obsessed with "America." With recourse to French structuralists and American critics of consumerism, he condemns the capitalist trend he identifies while admiring its seamless efficiency. Baudrillard makes clear the differences he sees as distinguishing France from the United States. He comes to criticize Europe and especially France, a nation-state burdened with cumbrous symbolic constructions and multi-layered urban spaces that he opposes to the lightness, speed, energy and circulation in the functionalist space of the United States (1991: 156–57).

It is the very failure of a revival of cultures based on existential paradigms and everyday spatial practices in the 1960s that, Baudrillard informs his readers, led him to the United States (which, as a would-be discoverer like the fictional Vespucci, he refers to as "America") where he found a "realized utopia," that is, a lack of perceived distinction between symbolic spaces with a sense of traditional culture and functionalism (1991: 156). Generalizing from the West Coast to the entire country, he declares that America has made a break with European utopia, especially that of 1968 with its emphasis on the everyday and on the non-distinction between culture and life. Because the country never knew the long phase of the accumulation of reality, it lives in perpetual simulation. It has erased all binary distinctions between city and country, nature and culture and, now even more so, it has evacuated entirely the bourgeois scene of representation. Space in America, Baudrillard declares peremptorily, is *not transcendental but simulated* (1991: 157). The opposition between the private and public arena has been overcome in favor of a homogeneous, efficient space of publicity, that is, of simulation. Unlike its European counterpart, the American city is not thinkable either as metaphoric or monumental. Instead of an anthropological city based on memory, the American city is a geometric space defined by circulation and not centralized through historical construction, as is a French or European city.

Baudrillard concludes his own fiction with a rhetorical flourish, noting that America has to be thought in terms of space but not of an existential territory. In America, people do not take refuge or find a sense of dwelling or *habitus* in everyday life. The desert spaces of California, what Deleuze and Guattari invoked to describe the effects of "smooth space" (1987), can be traversed in all possible directions. American cities are not referential (in respect to a territory, a memory or a history) but fictional. In Los Angeles, a city defined by circulation, cinema and freeways, a horizontal network replaces the sedimentation of organic substance. New York, built according to Rem Koolhaas after Coney Island, he senses (like many other French novelists and theorists) to be vertical (Koolhaas 1978). American cities are never far from the idea of a theme park consisting of new "anthropological" pockets that put many cultures on display. Baudrillard does not care to analyze the symbolic implications of such composite spaces in deference to his conclusion about how American cities, replete with wide open spaces, have clearly demarcated inner borders between different ethnic groups that in Europe are, inversely, complex and difficult to read. He declares emphatically that, if in America racism is spatial, in Europe it is philosophical. American thought, Baudrillard concludes triumphantly, is the thought of space (*la pensée de l'espace*).

Upon entering the disconnected and fictional universe of America he feels relieved of the unbearable weight of European culture. After denouncing the liquidation of geographical points of reference and the fictive media-spaces that replace them, Baudrillard now praises American functionalist spaces because they are devoid of European metaphysics. The highly mythologized "American space" is constructed from the critic's own fictions as well as from the images and illusions reflected to him by Americans themselves. For sure, the congestion he denounces on the highways in France had long ago, and long before Baudrillard visited, found its counterpart in Los Angeles and the rest of the country. Had he gone to the Northeast, especially, he would have found weighted spaces of memory he thought he had left behind. A quick stroll through Boston reveals a center, a panoply of monumental representations, congestion and the presence, as if in a time-lag, of streets laid out and paved for horse-drawn carriages in the era of colonial rule.

The contradictions of Baudrillard's fantasies are rampant in his observations of America. Let it be said that nonetheless he writes most tellingly during the advent of consumerism, information theory and a transformation of capitalism on the threshold of globalization. He chronicles the demise of the industrial, bourgeois society whose spaces are built upon hierarchies, moral values and interiority. Once the older system is unhinged, any resistance predicated on going back to the referent and a "real" that can now be historicized is hopelessly archaic. In the symbolic regime, space and time too have been eliminated from a system that is based on information and simultaneity. The aim today is control through normalization of the individual and the collective so as to assure the smooth, efficient functioning of global capitalism.

Baudrillard never developed the ecological dimension implied in his writings except to say that any notion of "dwelling," and with it of an existential territory, has gone with the wind. In *Simulations*, he dealt with instant feedback and information without really addressing what computers do to the experience of space. Before his death Baudrillard aimed to insert his critique at "the limit of a tendency" that would liquidate all resistances in the name of transnational capitalism. He took this aim for a reality, and in doing so he exposed the goals hidden under official rhetoric (which he calls double-dealing) imposed by media that "covers the earth." Yet is this tendency as universal as Baudrillard makes it out to be? And is its progress as undisputed as he claims? Are there resistances that either mitigate or alter this tendency? Is it possible to open micro-spaces in this urbanized world? And even before introducing resistances, are there simply other ways of reading this mainly American and Western world that Baudrillard is describing? Focusing increasingly on the loss of space and less on its transformation, the critic avoids thinking about how spaces could either be invented or made habitable. To tackle these questions, it is worth seeing if, next to the regime of simulation, it is still possible to delimit some residual existential and differential spaces that would not entirely be "vieilles vieilleries," as Rimbaud put it, in a world of digital images and signs. To do so we can turn to the anthropologist Marc Augé.

4

Marc Augé: Non-Places

> [I]ntelligence of space is less subverted by current upheavals (for soils and territories still exist, not just in the reality of facts on the ground, but even more in that of individual and collective awareness and imagination) than complicated by the spatial overabundance of the present.
>
> Augé, *Non-Places*

> [W]e live in a world we have not yet learned to look at. We have to relearn to think about space.
>
> Augé, *Non-Places*

The cover of the American edition of *The System of Objects* is illustrated with the chromium-plated grille of an American car of the 1960s, a behemoth vehicle that French filmmakers of the New Wave enjoyed inserting into the cityscapes of their films of the same decade. Taken from a neo-Pop painting, the cover signals to today's reader an affinity between the objects that called their culture into question and, in what followed, the hyperreal painters whose works displaying everyday objects in glaring clarity now seem, in view of what we see in "high def" and "blu-ray" television, to be diffusely mottled pastels. The surface effects of digital clarity that Baudrillard studied through a political lens seem remarkably close to what we witness on the televisual screens everywhere in our midst. What they display seems far from the mess and smudge of everyday life, unless, of course, we see them as the refuge of an artificial optical paradise. Such would seem to be the gap between an anthropologist's view of contemporary surface effects and what Baudrillard made of them in his spatial fictions. It is worth peering into the gap by way of what Marc Augé sees in the landmarks of France, especially of Paris, the city that for him is both an object of love and of close and protracted study.

The Anthropologist-Painter of Postmodern Life

An anthropologist in the tradition of Lévi-Strauss who reflects on anthropological spaces and subjectivity in traditional societies, Augé is marked by early preoccupations with the "space of others" that led him to do fieldwork on the Alladian peninsula of the Ivory Coast. After remarking how the palm oil industry contributed to the alteration of indigenous cultures, he returned to France to study new forms of relation and the new anthropological spaces in the urban environment of his childhood, adolescence and, now, later life. In Paris he coins the concept of an anthropology of the near—what Baudrillard might call an anti-ethnology—from the standpoint of new spaces and human relations in the France of the 1980s and 90s. Influenced by structural anthropology, and also through being a colleague and student of Michel de Certeau, Augé observes how acceleration in transportation and electronic communication and migrations have made an impact on his metropolis. In a variety of works (immediately striking is *Diana-Crash* [Augé et al. 1998], a study of the media-event that was Princess Diana's Ballard-like death in an automobile accident in a Parisian tunnel), he shows that the media are always keen to reduce society to an instantly legible and visible picture or tableau. However, this reduction (Augé appears to argue, *contra* Baudrillard) is thwarted by virtue of the conclusions that are drawn from the picture, especially how a public receives and refashions it. Like Augé himself, the public uses pictures and clichés as the raw material for a critical art of reading and seeing, even of analyzing the world around it.[1] The analysis of a society is always the result of a *double fiction*, both that of the subjects and that of the observer. It is at the intersection of the subjects' and the observer's illusions that notions of space and time and the subject are elaborated. A sense of space is gained through a manifold and co-extensive process of subjectivation and objectification. The "legibility" of the fiction is related to the idea of an *ordinary man* and of a society, however much they may seem "traditional" to the ethnologist, precisely located in geographical space and chronological time. If individuals are never completely detached from the society that traditionally assigns them a position from which they will gain subjectivity, they nonetheless always express the "totality" of the social body from a certain angle. Augé argues that even in the age of globalization, of the accelerated passage of information and transnational capitalism, no

1 The reader notes quickly that as anthropologist and "painter" of contemporary space Augé never stands for or sets himself above the public he addresses. Unlike Lefebvre, Augé does not project himself either as a magus or a bearer of truth to those who need to have it discerned for them. It is along these lines that the point of view and style of Augé's work is "minoritarian," insofar as it is not pitched to a pre-given public but uses its own forum to *invent* that public. The concept is developed in many of Deleuze and Guattari's writings (e.g., 1987: 280–320).

society can exist without at least a trace of alterity drawn through it. Or, as he puts it in *Le métro révisité* (2008), the "ethnologist of contemporary times and spaces," who rides the train going to and from Roissy airport, ought to stop at Châtelet-Les-Halles or the Gare du Nord to "attempt to hold in a single glance, as we had tried to do formerly in the villages of Africa or elsewhere, the ways of occupying space, the perennial modulations and the daily travels, the chronological regularities and the occasional perturbations" (56). A glimpse of totality is offered to the everyday subject (a rider who becomes a virtual ethnologist) passing through vastly different and quickly changing worlds.

Time and Space in Supermodernity

For the ethnologist who has witnessed in Africa a "world on the wane," a pressing question concerns not so much the disappearance of traditional space, time and the individual as learning to read the changes in a globalized world-space in which the media circulate information (if indeed it can be called information) at the speed of light. Augé exposes just this in *Non-Places*, published in France (under the title *Non-lieux*) in 1992, an essay that extends some of his other writings on the "anthropology of the near," such as *La traversée du Luxembourg* (1985) and both *Un ethnologue dans le métro* (1986) and its sequel, *Le métro révisité* (2008). What is, Augé begins by asking, the perception of traditional markers such as time and space in accelerated societies? What, today, happens to the subject or, as he puts it, the individual? Using very general and almost universalizing terms, Augé writes about French—and what seem to be territorial—perceptions as they are restructured to the European context. He notes that, with an overabundance of events, time is no longer a principle of intelligibility. Technological progress is said to go hand-in-hand with moral progress but continued wars tell us otherwise.[2] Given the gradual fade of monumental history from today's horizon, how can we make sense of what informs contemporary time? On the one hand, discarding the great teleological narratives of the past, the neo-Braudelian historians now focus heavily on the everyday, from the family to private life, and on public arenas as places of memory. On the other hand, people develop an interest in obsolete forms and want to

2   On this point his aptly titled *La guerre des rêves* (1998) is pertinent. It studies how the imagination is a contested battleground wherever contemporary life gets saturated with media-driven images; it anticipates the later essay on the death of Princess Diana (1998).

revive the past artificially. Studies of the past focus on the everyday, the family and private life to show people what they no longer are. They see what has changed in them or, as Augé, alluding to Pierre Nora's *Lieux de mémoire*, puts it: "Within this difference, there is a flash of identity that is established always against a place of memory" (1995: 26). Corresponding to the decline is a diminution of reference to Sartrean (existential) and Marxist (material-historical) assessments of the post-war period. In both strains truth was claimed to be universal. In place of these points of reference came a variety of "competing" claims to universalism that have fractured or radically altered given coordinates of contemporary time and space.

If modernity could be seen as the illusion of an evolution that resembles progress, supermodernity or *surmodernité* (the term Augé coins to avoid what he sees as postmodern pessimism) is the end of this process. With the advent of teletechnologies and the increased availability of intercontinental transportation, time now consists in a jolting acceleration of history. Augé declares that today, with global media, every moment becomes living history, which consists of a series of events understood by a large number of people. The overabundance of events in the twentieth century, the result mainly of technologies of transmission and of memory, as Claude Lévi-Strauss anticipated in *Tristes tropiques* (1955), can be treated as a question of scale. Since information moves more quickly, an augmentation and acceleration of events tends to rob them of meaning. The Parisian subway, which once rolled on its rubber wheels back and forth from Neuilly to Vincennes, now invites its riders to imagine themselves transported, like the name of the new line (number 14) from Tolbiac to Madeleine, at the speed of a "meteor."

In view of a proliferation of spaces in built environments, Augé asks how in the age of supermodernity meaning can be given to society in a greater (and accessible) world felt to be without a grounding principle or final goal. Instead of promoting a feeling of resignation à la Baudrillard (who informs people that they are the unsuspecting victims of a new elite and the media in a system based solely on profit), Augé summons a need for a new and positive demand for meaning. He seems to have us ask ourselves where we are and why. Why here and not there? If *there* is immediately accessible from *here*, can places be defined by the time needed to travel from here to there? The seeming diminution of distance and space leads to the idea that the world is open to humans and that it is legible for one and all. Yet far from simply abolishing time and space, the transformations that technologies bring about should force humans to re-evaluate the perceptions of their basic cultural coordinates: when and where they are born into what kind of world; who is proximate and who or what is other; how to negotiate the inherited "sense" of a given culture and how to take creative "liberties" with it, and so on.[3] The intelligibility of space is not lost; it too has been complicated by an overabundance and also by a differential notion of scale.

Augé studies older ways of thinking time and space in his own autobiographical sketches. They are implied to have had currency up to the end of the Second World War, whose unfathomable and traumatic events soon become known and are packaged and circulated in the regime of electronic images and satellite television. The past remains obstinately present and in need of being *both* remembered and forgotten.[4] The anthropologist examines how a universe created by satellite television serves as a substitute for a previous one based on historical and structural referents (the dominion of "sense") in which it was founded. What were real symbolic territories, localized in time and space, are now replaced by images of communication, in other words by a fictional universe of recognition. Recognition replaces personal and empirical knowledge with little more than acknowledgment that information has been registered. Observation is no longer direct but relayed through digital images and signs, many of which Augé now sees flashing everywhere in the urban complex.

During the era of modernity the concern of the ethnologist had been to delineate signifying spaces in the world of societies identified with cultures conceived as complete, and within which individuals and groups were considered to be a mere expression. This assumption reflected the ethnographer's illusions as much as those of the people themselves. *Surmodernité* is a critical outcome of modernism that had been based on an outworn sense of relativism. The reality of today's spatial and temporal "overabundance" is a greater urban concentration, increased movement of hybrid populations and the proliferation of what Augé, altering a term coined by Certeau, calls "non-places." To merit a name, a place need not have been a piece of lived or experienced space. The absence of any past in the non-place results in a paradox: at the very time humans are made to think about the unity of terrestrial—or global—

---

3 In *Le métier d'anthropologue* (2006: 40–60), Augé defines "sense" as that which defines and confines activity in a culture and "liberty" as the creative force (often of transgression) that inheres in it

4 In *Les formes de l'oubli* (1998) he notes that without oblivion we could not live an everyday life. Suggesting that memory could traumatize and immobilize the everyday, he argues for a balance of memory and praxis. Yet in *Casablanca* (2007) Augé jars his memory in order to recall where he was and how he reacted to the Second World War.

space, a feeling of vacuity or superfluity ("Why am I in the world?") prompts demands for new existential relations with chosen places. Like Baudrillard, albeit with a different conclusion, Augé proposes to engage an "anti-ethnology" that will take up the formations of new cultures and civilizations, under the impact of technological and demographic change, along with different coordinates of time and space. He cautions that supermodernity is not the regime in which we think we live, and as a result declares that we have to be rid of former existential illusions and relearn how to think about space (1995: 36).[5]

The Individual in Accelerated Society

How is the question: the individual or the "ego" has returned in anthropology, somewhat like the repressed, in works where the "I" has become a self-authenticating shifter. Augé argues that attention should be given to the reconstruction of places and to singularities in counterpoint to what an intellectual elite would call world-culture as given through acceleration and delocalization (1995: 40). The anthropologist proposes to look at the three entities—time, space and the individual—in order to learn how to read new complexities rather than simply to consign a lost modernity to history. No matter what may be the meaning that we assign to our moment, facts—e.g., birth, even marriage and death more total than those that Mauss had categorized—will not disappear but make sense again in a different world.

Augé exposes and summarizes the relation of the individual to time and space in anthropology while treating them as components of each other. Critical of modernity, he also dismisses as a kind of "narrow hermeneutics" that which allowed interpreters, of a postmodern text-oriented school (which he sees represented by James Clifford), to construct their identities through the studies they make of others. In Western societies the individual wants to be a world to himself or herself. Yet the individual is always affected by collective history. When individuals notice that their identity is shaped by collective forces, any identification or osmosis with the world becomes improbable, even though the production of individual or individuated meaning is still

---

5 How to relearn to think about space is the topic of Wim Wenders' film *Lisbon Story* (1994), much admired by Augé. The film features a disillusioned filmmaker and his assistant who relearn to look at the world and note that even in an era of electronic equipment and commercialism, it is still possible to make images and open spaces.

necessary. The important question is how to think and situate the individual both after Mauss's concept of the ordinary man (whose life attests to total social facts) *and* after a postmodern, culturalist, indeed text-oriented school of self-involved inquiry. Michel de Certeau, Augé claims, found the individual in the tricks he or she enacts to circumvent the constraints of the state on the threshold of globalization.[6] Certeau's "subjects" were a multiplication of the ordinary—or average—man whom he opposed to the elite. The elite has had decision-making power to make the ordinary man obey and consume as he or she would wish (1995: 38). By means of tactics or tricks, in his exercise of liberty Augé's "average man," like Certeau's *homme ordinaire*, would also defy this scheme and become a producer of space.

Place and space become major categories for people wherever identity and reciprocal relations are countenanced. They condition the usage of the "I" (or "we") according to a variety of contexts. In traditional societies, place is where people live and dwell; it cultivates ancestors, harbors its spirits and remains a humanistic anchor; it is a site of invention both for those who live in it as well as for those who decipher its various human geographies. For that reason its veracity is a function of the *fictions* its users make of it. A sense of "reality" is still based on the fiction of a closed world in which every event can be made accessible to discourse or, simply put, made legible. In more traditional cultures, public and private spatial arrangements express the identity of a group. The group, though often diverse in origin, is united by the identity of place. It defends itself not only against external but also internal threats, so that the language of identity retains a meaning and allows the fantasy of a founding place to shape an illusion of self-identity. Fragile and always subject to adjustment, the image of a closed world is not a lie but a productive myth inscribed in the soil. Both the inhabitants and the ethnographer-observer create a semi-illusion of its cultural surface that is subject to the vicissitudes of history, mobility and fluctuations of borders and spaces.

At the same time, the ethnologist is not simply the "I" or the "we" who compiles, registers and translates the expression of a closed society and the place of the social individual who would "typically" live within its borders. Anthropological place, Augé declares, is a concrete and symbolic construction that does not allow for the contradictions of social

6 For Marcel Mauss, a "total social fact" (in French, a *fait social total*) is a "fact" or activity that has implications throughout society in economic, legal, political and religious spheres. The gist of this reflection is at the basis of his essay, *The Gift* (Mauss 2002).

life but serves as reference for those it assigns to a position (1995: 53). Anthropological places have a principle of meaning for insiders and a principle of intelligibility for outsiders. Places whose analysis yields meaning or offers a compass point for orientation do so because of the inhabitants themselves. Place is discerned where it is *invested* with meaning. It is that in which relations are acted out. To be born is to be born in a place, the place of birth constituting an identity by strong virtue of a number of pre-given rules of residence. A child is situated in an overall configuration on the soil he or she shares with others, and thus place, as a locus of dwelling and living, is made manifest through identity and relation that, being both past and present, constitute it as a living history. Consisting of a set of references, many of which may change at different hours of the day (a square, for example, may become a market place), a territory is constitued through the sum of the ways in which its inhabitants mythologize it.

In turn, Augé glosses the distinctions made by Merleau-Ponty between anthropological and geometric spaces to argue that a strict division between the two is impossible to maintain. Even an elementary social space consists of geometrical lines and their many intersections. When translated into everyday life, it becomes an anthropological space of roads, paths, crossroads and open spaces that include markets as well as religious and political centers, the implication being that it is defined by ever-existential relations whose forms become those into which individuals are born, grow and, as it were, "find" themselves. What is existential can be thus institutional, insofar as both market and hearth exist through contracts and respect for procedures in which political and economic spaces are mixed. Augé continually emphasizes the diversity of human worlds which cannot be subsumed under the myth of a single universal truth. Beyond these roads, centers and towns, he underlines, other humans entertain different relations with space and time. If what is here and what is there, or what is qualified as identity or alterity, is at the heart of all spatial relations they are also at the crux of history, the field of study and of experience against which anthropology traditionally defines the principles of its discipline.

Space and Non-Place

From the beginning of his career Augé has located his ethnography in a frame of history. In 1992, the time at which the concept of the non-place is launched, Paris is considered to be "the center of French space."

Similarly, much as we read in Proust, the novelist who inspires Augé's later work on memory and oblivion, each province or region outside of the capital has a center marked by a defining monument. The spatial layout of all cities and towns is—or at least was—similar. The *mairie* or town hall, the church and the market place are in the center. Commemoration services establish rituals, such as July 14, the national holiday, or November 11, the day of the Armistice of 1918 that has now officially become Veterans' Day. New towns in France and the *banlieue* are often criticized for lacking a center (Augé 1995: 66).[7] The national space made visible on a Michelin map consists of a cluster of centers and the roads that link them. Every settlement is the center of a space made meaningful through comparative features highlighted in tourist manuals. Yet, amidst the "old" places that define the nation, new signs of "twinning" (*jumelage*) signify the integration of France in a greater European Union.

A town's claim to history is now displayed on signboards, the result of a reorganization of space by means of highways and bypasses. The signs are usually made to attract tourists. They link the measure of today's effectiveness (a bypass) with a touch of history and a longing for a bygone past (*à visiter éventuellement*, "to visit eventually," as the *Guide Michelin* puts it). History is always rooted in the soil, and indeed the monument serves as a guarantee of its authenticity. The names of roads, like those of Parisian subway stations, remind people of the past by alluding to history of the kind learned in secondary schools. However, the relation with history has been de-socialized at the price of greater aestheticization. People no longer live in Paris; they commute. Younger generations, immigrants or tourists have little inkling of local history, nor are they disposed to inform themselves about it (Augé 1996). The transformation from historical to aesthetic space is partially attributable to André Malraux, novelist and hero of the Resistance who, when he became Minister of Culture under Charles de Gaulle, crafted isolated French towns into museums established so as to figure in new networks of pilgrimage and economic development. A telling example: Malraux had designated Sarlat-la-Canède in the Dordogne to be rebuilt as a replica of a medieval town. This has been done, not only to invigorate the local economy, but also to link Sarlat to nearby Montignac, the hamlet that now welcomes flocks of tourists who visit the replica of Lascaux, which

---

7 Life in a new town was aptly shown by Eric Rohmer in his film *Boyfriends and Girlfriends* (1987). Ironically, the buildings and the neighborhood of Cergy-Pontoise where the film was shot have now been taken over by immigrant groups, introducing further spatial transformations. For problems with space in the *banlieue*, see Azouz Begag, Chapter 2.

in turn leads them to the newly minted Museum of Prehistory only a few kilometers away, near Font-de-Gaume, which figures as a deviation from the major route leading the traveler from Paris to Bordeaux. Malraux had signs erected to beckon tourists to come and look at the past splendor of their cultural heritage. Today an occasional irony is found where these signs are staked, often at the edge of town, specifically near the *cités* (housing projects) where immigrants are concentrated, or near shopping malls and airports. The pre-modern figure of a continuous temporality that in the Middle Ages was built around a church and a bell tower is now a matter of imagination and a feeling of sublimity.

All things being equal, a *place* then is at once spatial (relational), temporal (historical) and linked to identity (individual). The perceived elision of history allows Augé to call a space that does not consist of social relations—because social relations are deeply embedded in time—one of the principal attributes of the non-place. The absence of social relations defines the character of the airport, shopping mall and supermarket. While places have specific positions in the eyes of those who move about them, non-places are in themselves mobile and ephemeral, linked to networks—the subway, the taxi, the interstate highway—that make them accessible. They all create solitary individuals who, while they pass through them, are bereft of identity or of existential relations with what is there. Yet, Augé concludes, non-places never exist in pure form. Places reconstitute themselves in them and new relations are formed (1995: 79).

Non-places, the measure of our time, are so problematic that the distinction, formerly essential to Michel de Certeau's doublets of place versus space or strategy versus tactic, now submits to significant modification. Place no longer refers to the soil and does not order people's identity or their relations. It is shown to be a soft realm of contractual "liberty under surveillance" (Augé 2008: 67) in which "the individuality of the consuming individual" in the subway, airport or supermarket is a "passive individuality limited by the financial means at one's disposal and the gamut of products put before his or her eyes" (66–67). Time produces an overabundance of events while space, helped by the media, proliferates and circulates as new places, such as "leisure spaces" or "sports spaces," or the inside of a car of a given brand name (say, *espace Renault*).

Neither places nor symbolic spaces of place, they are what Augé calls non-symbolized surfaces of the planet or non-symbolic spaces of non-places. "The serene and disincarnated voices in airports never fail to give us a first taste of paradise as it is habitually imagined," notes the narrator of Augé's first novel, *La mère d'Arthur* (2005: 69). These "soft" places

that we so readily occupy, and that we enjoy in paging through the maga-
zines we extract from the seatbacks in front of us when we travel by air,
project images of leisure (cars, boats), of tourist areas (resorts, beaches)
and of items to consume. They have become abstract signs. Much of the
space that Augé's traveler occupies in the novel is a non-place. The solitary traveler contemplates landscapes—of Costa Rica and the suburbs of
Paris—with which he shares no relation, history or identity. The movement of travel—and what travel is not a form of tourism?—underscores
the fact that solitude is at the basis of our relations with space and place.
To this solitude there corresponds an emptying of individuality or subjectivity. Supermodernity, Augé concludes, corresponds to an emptying of
consciousness. In the non-place, symbolic relations give way to contractual relations while links between individuals and places are established
through words that often evoke images. Proper or common names may
evoke certain desires (Paris, love; the Caribbean, sun, sex, sea; France,
fashion, gastronomy) that are elicited according to paradigms of control.[8]

Non-places can be understood as clichés in which the words that name
them do not open a gap between a deictic function and the lost myth of
reference. The word creates the image and produces the myth, thus
implying that "real" non-places exist only in words. On the French
highway, in conjunction with the example of Sarlat-la-Canède, the historical landscape may be concealed, but the culture of the billboard that
punctuates the itinerary sanitizes the past. National roads of this kind
used to be tied quasi-organically to social life. Now they are reduced to
cavalcades of texts and images that fabricate today's "average man" who
is the user of roads, airports or automatic tellers and who has only
contractual relationships with them. In a non-place, people are no longer
practitioners. They become users to whom are offered an allure of individualization. An organic anthropological place, unlike that in which
simulation is the case, individualizes identities through local references
and rules. Augé echoes Certeau when he writes that in an anthropological place, people are travelers. In a non-place, they become tourists or
passengers who have no shared identity.[9] They have a contractual relationship with these non-places and are only what they experience in their
present role. They have to give proof that the contract is respected. Augé's
timely example of the immigration desk is noteworthy: in order to pass
the border travelers are obliged to show their passports to police and

8 Such is what comes out of Laurent Cantet's *Vers le sud* (2005), a film based on a
   novel with the same title by Dany Laferrière (2006) in which American women
   spend their summer in a resort in Haiti under the Duvalier regime.
9 Michel de Certeau reaches a similar conclusion (1984: 111–14).

customs officials. What if the person is an immigrant, especially if he or she is illegal? How does she or he compare with a tourist? For Augé it is significant that any person who enters the space of non-place is relieved of his or her usual determinants of relation and identity. The proof of contract is a mere access code. We can ask, however, if humans are simply leaving behind their usual determinants when they leave an existential (or anthropological) space and find themselves, where they are often employed, in a living situation whose defining character resembles a non-place? Are the determinants not irrevocably affected and undermined by this shift away from the soil in stark contrast to the new place? Augé seems to indicate that wherever we are we shuttle back and forth between places and non-places. Yet we may wonder whether these places are spatially as separate as he makes them out to be and whether the two do not intertwine in such a way that new coordinates of space and time as well as other subjectivities are created (say, of the immigrant experience that Begag had taken up in his inquiries).

In reality, Augé concedes, it becomes hard to distinguish between place, non-place and space. Like most of his fellow travelers, he ascertains that even today words can still take root in the surviving and diverse anthropological places where people try to construct at least part of their everyday lives. Even if non-places are more fashionable—in Augé's words, *elite*—many humans explicitly long for an everyday life in which, however minimal they may be, existential choices are possible. Ecological spaces are sometimes felt to be found in challenged parts of the city or, as Assouz Begag had shown, in less-developed countries.[10] People in these places of "resistance" or backward places are often—and wrongly—perceived as experiencing a plenitude of which others are bereft.[11] The fetishization of poverty is a familiar theme. However, it is clear that, unless poverty becomes too debilitating, anthropological spaces can survive in poor communities, at the antipodes of non-places, while in affluent societies contractual relations among solitary and self-involved "individuals" increasingly prevail, challenging more traditional concepts of habitability.

10 This nostalgia leads to questionable forms of tourism like visits to the street children in the train stations of Bombay, to the *favelas* of Rio de Janeiro or housing estates in the Parisian *banlieue*.
11 This is evidenced in Certeau's ordinary people, Patrick Keiller's film *London* (1992), parts of Salman Rushdie's *Satanic Verses* (1988) and many writings on the French *banlieue*.

Place and Space in a Global Era: "Rimbaud's Mother"

In *La mère d'Arthur*, his first official novel, Augé reflects on how place
and singularity may still be possible in the global era. A missing person,
Nicolas, has staged his flight from his wife and family as a disappearance. In his search for Nicolas, the narrator, who is his close friend, flies
to Costa Rica where he meets a French woman who was Nicolas' lover;
her present lover, a refugee from a German university who—with echoes
of Nabokov's *Lolita*—collects butterflies; and the daughter whom the
woman's dead husband had adopted from Somalia, a contemporary
Lolita of sorts, who is about to go off to study at Harvard University.[12]
While in Costa Rica, the narrator enjoys fine Burgundy wine and French
cuisine. The narrative implicitly—in the very area of difference between
the non-place and the maze of interrelated fantasies of connectedness (not
unlike Baudrillard)—takes a wry view of the stifling atmosphere of
French familial space. The itinerary passes through many non-places,
which are both replicated and countered by those in Costa Rica, in the
shade of the palm trees (of the order of those in advertisements for facial
creams) where he meets the "family" with whom he stays. Made of a
new set of relations, this family does not have a common language and
is not inscribed in a common soil. Just as mangoes from the Antilles
invade French supermarkets, so also are French products (including the
narrator himself) found in Costa Rica, where tourists buy souvenirs in
traditional local markets. The narrative that leads back to a psychiatric
ward on the outskirts of Paris leaves the reader in a state of charmed and
uneasy ambivalence.

   La mère d'Arthur tells us that territories are disappearing along with
the nuclear family and its constructions of center and periphery, here and
elsewhere, the everyday and exotic as well as symbolic places and history.
The characters move amidst abstract spaces made up of clichéd, non-
referential words and images in which logos and soundbites tell them
who they are. The recognition of their alienation is vital to the empirical
knowledge that they gain from the museum (the city of Paris), touristic
utopias (Costa Rica) or the asylum (in the suburbs of Paris) where the
narrator and his other ultimately find themselves.

   Anticipating his novel, Augé opened *Non-Places* with a short allegory
of the contemporary "ordinary" Frenchman, conspicuously called M.
Dupont, the Gallic equivalent of Mr. Smith. Much as will the narrator

12 She was turned down by French universities, an indirect criticism of a discrimi-
   nating French educational system.

of *La mère d'Arthur*, the latter moves through a series of non-places (highway, tollbooth, an airport lounge and a duty-free shop), before beginning a journey of recognition to Asia by airplane. This Frenchman could be an anthropologist en route to a conference in one of the usual non-places—from the Singapore Marriott to the Hong Kong Hilton—where business "takes place." He has the privilege of moving quickly (once he removes his belt and shoes, passes through security and retrieves his X-rayed effects from the conveyor belt) and of having the means to trot about the globe. His mobility allows him to palliate the crushingly soft solitude of the areas of transit, and his own unchecked existential baggage permits him to take a distance from the non-places in which he finds himself. Some of it is literature, or at least the canon of French literature that he has learned and that he knows how, by virtue of the soothing style of his writing, to manipulate for a critical pleasure of his own. In *La mère d'Arthur*, the text of the account is the very *space* Augé invents from the descriptions of the *non-place*. The literary heritage that allows him to turn Rimbaud, by way of a spoonerism, into *Robin* (*des bois*, or Robin Hood) and to make substance from the virtual relation that he might have had with the "other" (whether his friend Nicolas or the other personages) attests to the crucial vitality of myth and story-telling, of wit and invention that, in a Certallian manner, alters even non-places into ecological spaces.

In the Paris Subway

More recently, in reflecting on the changes he has witnessed in the Parisian subway in the passage of twenty-two years since *Un ethnologue dans le métro* (1986), a nuanced sense of space and place marks Augé's impressions of the refurbished stations, the commercial centers that are found at some of the "hubs" where the RATP and the RER intersect, where a general ambiance of automation and telesurveillance is felt amidst the throngs of people who pass through their corridors. Until now, the reader has had the indelible impression that the *métro* had stood in opposition to the non-place because it was a world in which, despite its closure, spatial stories could be plotted and experienced by millions of users of limited means. It was a place that easily transmuted into space simply because the rider could choose mental itineraries while building fantasies from the names of the lines and of their stations. The toponyms are more than raw material for a gazetteer of illusions about the greatness of France. At the Austerlitz stop, Augé reminds the reader, no

Waterloo is to be found further down the line. It is up to the rider to imagine areas in and out of this world. The cliffs of the Côte sauvage and the prehistoric menhirs would go with the Breton space of "Filles du Calvaire." And so the metro is a place where the vague stirring of community (all of Paris, in its entire spectrum of cultures and of peoples) can be felt in the collective idea of "embarking" and of "disembarking" at one stop or another.

In 2008, however, Augé calls the metro an *auxiliary* to the RER, which brings its riders farther and farther away, to places—namely, Roissy-Aéroport Charles de Gaulle—from which, with wherewithal enough, they can be taken out of this world. It is not the closed entity it had been because it serves the end of a means to many non-places, and at its principal axes, as at La Défense, les Halles (which has seven levels underground) and Montparnasse or the Gare du Nord, the metro is a site for commercial activity of the kind known in non-places: stores and windows, "arcades" for our age that are implied to be quite different from those that fascinated Walter Benjamin. Non-places as they have become, they still belong to the very real and productive oscillation between a place and a space. Yet, if they continue to harbor a presence of community and, as the movement of Augé's words tells us, a strong impression of life, this communal space is now in movement, mobile and ephemeral:

> Inside of the moving wagons and in the stations where we change lines or means of transport *public space affirms its existence* in an eventually contradictory manner. Public space, if by that we mean the space in which everyone meets one another, but also the *abstract space* in which public opinion is formed, is identified to a large degree with the space of public transport [...] Thus the feeling of insecurity is latent, and collective stirrings can at any moment, on the occasion of a police-check or a late train, throw the system into disorder. The "France of diversity" that everyday is clogging our arteries *experiences* the weight and resistance of everyday life. (2008: 61–62)

In this line of reflection the place that had been the metro retains some of its presence. It affirms that a sense of living and a territorializing subjectivity are strong and true but also threatened by a growing sense of insecurity. As we move ahead, in the abstraction of flashing signs, "simulacra," and gloss, solitude increasingly defines the non-places Augé observes from a moving train rather than from the platform. A more static concept of an overabundance of spaces gives way to transport and mobility in space. If symbolic and territorial spaces still exist, they are complicated by the media and an ever-more accelerated society. The subway Augé revisits in 2008 might be contracted as a "non-place-not-yet." It offers some access to space through what it does to our consciousness of motion and locomotion, and its history remains intact, however much it may be aestheticized, be it in a place-name such as Montparnasse-Bienvenüe (the toponym including the surname of the great engineer of the metro) or a secret memory-place.

The non-place owes something to the artists of the hyperreal, noted at the beginning of this chapter, who inspired reflection on the character of life in the 1960s and beyond. While Baudrillard has summed up much of the effect of consumer culture and shown what it does in a global perspective, Augé prefers not to divine—but only hint at—the future of the non-place. That task has devolved upon his friend and colleague, Paul Virilio. Virilio, writing not long ago of Augé's gift of *premonition* of the character of life ahead of us, brings speed into the equation that Augé drew when he revisited the Parisian subway in 2008. We have seen that now and again, more frequently now than at the time he wrote *Non-Places*, in addition to means of transportation, Augé deals with "fast" media—television, e-mail, e-commerce, iPods, cell phones, text messages —and, to a degree, with the ways the character of anthropological space is changed. What he *implies* to be their effects happens to be the topic of Virilio's work on space in respect to its perception through movement. Augé's legacy of premonition is a logically real and vital place from which to begin the chapter that follows.

5

Paul Virilio: Speed Space

> After having lost the street in the nineteenth century, people are now also losing their voice.
>
> Paul Virilio

> Speed is not simply a matter of time. Speed is also space-time. It is an environment that is defined in equal measure by space and by time.
>
> Armitage (ed.), *Virilio Live*

In his recent homage to Marc Augé, Paul Virilio asserts that the author of *Non-Places* has turned anthropology into a science responsible less for reconstituting traditional cultures than for scaffolding an *art of premonition*. The ethnologist of today can no longer study societies "without history" but, rather, the fragile state of a world in which chronological time has telescoped to the state of instantaneity. Space, like the wild ass's skin in Balzac's *La Peau de chagrin*, has shrunk beyond belief. Virilio, whose brilliantly delphic writings hover between the messianic and the titanic, finds in Augé a friend who senses the effects that the acceleration of information have on subjectivity. The supermodernity (*surmodernité*) of which Augé writes "is surely the combined effect of the acceleration of history and of a shrinkage of geographical space giving occasion [...] to both 'an individualization of destinies' and to diverse destinations of action" (Virilio 2008: 100). The effect, he notes, is that individuals now owe their existential being to a condition of solitude. They find themselves in a state of accelerated delocalization, which is exactly what the anthropologist discovered in his own premonitions. Virilio finds in the anthropologist's labors an attempt to gain a distance from himself while within his field of inquiry a tension reigns between premonition (*pressentiment*) and resentment (*ressentiment*). Virilio's intergalactic fantasies are born of the tension. He writes that everything is happening today as if we were seeing the world as had the astronauts who landed on the moon forty years ago:

> Before this viewpoint of "extrapolarization" the anthropologist of premonition risks quickly being transformed into one of profound resentment in view of the black utopia of disaster that constrains humanity to evacuate the places (*les lieux*) in order to take exile God-knows-where, far from here-

78

and-now, in the outer world of cybernetic illuminism; in a solar cult no longer of light as once before, but of speed; in a new absolute of a century that would be far from that of the "Enlightenment" as everyone already foresees it (*le pressent*). It would be the century of *darkness* of postmodern obscurantism in which the search of our astronomers for *black matter* and its *concealed energy*—said to be responsible for universal expansion—would indicate above all a denial of the visible and the manifest in favor of the unperceived, the unexpected, the unsayable qualities of these "clouds of unknown knowledge" that our wise doctors mocked not long ago. (2008: 102, my translation)

In these words, of a style and substance of their own, at once opaque and illuminating, it is difficult to discern where Augé ends and Virilio begins. Virilio uses the resemblance of a *lien* (a bond) to a *lieu* (a place) to have the one displace the other. Space, what would be calibrated in the diurnal conditions of science and Enlightenment, is now made menacingly obscure. Light is not what enlightens, what is "shed" or "cast" upon an object to make it known, but rather pure velocity. Virilio's words signal that dark matter can be construed to be both oil and the black holes left behind when it is extracted from the earth—but also the India ink the ethnologist draws from his well of inspiration to write what he does. The drift of Virilio's style indicates that our world is plummeting into a black hole.

The relation he establishes with Augé's spatial thought implies much about his own work on space in our time. The French thinkers discussed so far are haunted by what they perceive as the loss of both existential territory and the conflicted world of the wars into which they were born. They define this existential space as relational, as gestural and as lived. Loss of human agency results from sanctioned imposition of templates on everyday life correlative with the order of a new consumerism that the electronic media mobilize on a global scale. They all concur that objects are further removed from the signs that name them; that figures are replaced by abstractions; that a tenor of the real or "reality" is lost or simulated. They remark that a disciplinary society, based on a division between inside and outside and stratified by distinct social hierarchies, gives way to another, based on new forms of control affiliated with increasing urbanization, where center and periphery or beginning and end are indiscernible, and in which power circulates, unbeknownst to us, in myriad worldwide networks.

The geographies that new technologies of consumerism have created can be perceived to be both utopian and dystopian. Individuals are said to be set free from their assigned places in symbolic orders and to reside, as one sociologist (Conley 2009) puts it, "elsewhere," looking away from inherited points of reference that had assigned meaning to everyday life.

The new or even "hyperexistential" freedom is shown coming at the cost of a Faustian bargain. Erosion of symbolic relations gives individuals a false sense of personal freedom. New hierarchies are based on economic status and money, and so fast and pervasively that the "dawn of liberation" Henri Lefebvre glimpsed on the horizon in his later writings is quickly receding.

Speed Space

Virilio obsessively chronicles the transformations of space according to the evolution of capitalism from its early phases to its current character. What we call the "market" under capitalism has always been coordinated with the military sphere. Engineers in the armed forces work for the ends of *speed*. Speed is a form of war in which, headlong, sideways or in retreat, the fastest wins. His early "Métempsychose du passager," published in a review dedicated to space in which Virilio, Certeau, Baudrillard, Augé and others participated, argues that our world has witnessed a progression from a metabolic to a mechanical vehicle, that is, from war on foot to war on horseback and, now, to war engineered by machines that go from Gatling guns to drones directing laser-guided missiles (1977: 11–15). Virilio offers a sweeping history, beginning with more detailed attention to the nineteenth century, which he sees as a backdrop to the impact of technologies on the experience of space and time since the Second World War.

He looks at the condition of existential space through the filter of traumatic childhood memories. His early *Bunker Archeology* recalls the moments before D-Day when Allied planes flew over the Atlantic Wall the Germans had erected along the western coast of France. The "bunker" strategy had not accounted for air power reaching over and beyond an otherwise impregnable line of defense. It was an event, Virilio says, that irremediably changed relations of humans to space. Before disappearing into cyberspace, war was first taken from the earth to the sea and eventually to the air.[1] As of that moment, limits cross *inside* a territory that can no longer defend itself from the outside. From there the cultural theorist traces a history of space from the impact of technologies deployed in the Cold War to those in what he calls Pure War (based on atomic deterrence), to today's global world living under the shadow of the "information bomb."

1 The passage on the capitalist appropriation of smooth space from *Speed and Politics* (1986: 70) is developed by Deleuze and Guattari. See Chapter 6.

Recognizing the successive stages of the development of capitalism (along the lines of Lefebvre's schemes that undergird his *Production of Space*), Virilio argues that, nonetheless, military invention remains the driving force of technological development shaping our experience of space. The military sector drives technological development, coupled first with the military–industrial (along with the sphere of manufacture) and now with the informational (or technological) complex. When the military shifts its strategy from wars that oppose two armies to that of preventive war (what Baudrillard called deterrence and what the Bush administration more recently called "pre-emptive" attack and conquest) involving the population at large, space is defined by insecurity and even by fear.

A critic of consumerism, Baudrillard focused on economic exchange in the cybernetic lexicon of the relation between "input and output." He noticed that an acceleration of goods and information, enabled by transportation and electronic technology, resulted in the compression of space and the altering of long-held forms of symbolic exchange. He did not quite see acceleration as speed, a concept that alters the experience of space, time and subjectivity in general (Virilio 1986). The innovation in Virilio's work is found in the claim that speed itself is a *milieu*, an environment, a setting, and not a calibration of time passed in movement between one place and another. Speed is space-time, that is, an environment in which inertia is felt within greater movement on the globe or even in galactic space. Today the measure or mean of speed is that of light (roughly 186,000 miles per second), a velocity that furnishes a metric for the passage of information. Just as cinema, a medium based on light, utterly changed the ways we understand the ambient world, more often than not technologies of illumination have changed subjectivity, which Virilio understands to be the process of living in a world whose rhythms, firmly based on the alteration of diurnal and nocturnal phases, are now—beyond the dreams of the Enlightenment—almost entirely diurnal. It does not take a quantum leap for Virilio to infer that speed leads simultaneously to the demise of the nation-state and to a view of the city that has been entirely transformed under the impact of electronic transmission and the information bomb. Detached from the nation-state on which it was built, the urban milieu, the matrix for much of the world's population, has lost the territorial aspect of the *polis* that defines the citizen as such.[2]

2 Paul Virilio, "La ville surexposée," in *L'espace critique* (1984; in English as *The Lost Dimension* [1991]). See also "The Overexposed City" (in *Zone*, n.d. and Leach 1992: 381–90).

Wars are won and lost according to various measures of speed. The siege mentality (associated with bunkers) depends on duration, on a time in which days and months tick by slowly and inexorably while borders are defended with artillery. Virilio sees how the quick and often massive strike made outside of a classically defined territory changes "the rules of the game." Since 1977, the date of the publication in France of *Politics of Speed*, Virilio has written on the etymology of the French term speed, *vitesse*, and its derivatives of *vie* and *vis* that denote life and force (1991: 70). A virtue of attack and control, velocity is the essence that defines the experience of space. When speed is harnessed to a controlling apparatus (whether ideological or institutional), the existential space of those who live in milieus governed by technologies of speed is progressively lost; this is shown, he argues, by the way military takeovers took place in Latin America in the 1970s (chronicled in *Popular Defense and Ecological Struggles* [1990]).

Virilio set a wake-up call for critics and theorists as early as 1984 when—in the same year that William Gibson published his first cyber-novel *Neuromancer*, as the critic now likes to point out—he declared [in *L'espace critique*, translated as *The Lost Dimension* (1991)] that *space* has become "critical" and should henceforth become a concept and merit treatment as such. He follows a fairly standard argument: as soon as cyberneticians measure the passage of information according to the speed of light, Newtonian physics gives way to Einsteinian relativity. Time and space become compressed. Even though ten minutes are required for a particle or a wave of light to travel from the sun to the earth, the sheer velocity of the process cannot be imagined. It is so rapid that we must take the speed of light on faith. In *The Art of the Motor* (1995), which shows that, since the birth of cinematography, art is always in movement, Virilio also follows the path of analogy by which the computer is said to bring obsolescence to writing. By extension (despite its association with *res extensa*), the entire universe is abstracted when converted into discrete units; when digitized and virtualized, reality itself (exceeding Baudrillard's idea of simulation as the basis of the real) becomes a mode of accelerated transport. When metaphors move at the speed of light the real and its existential dimensions, which had been so important for humans, are diminished. Instead of *simulation* (Baudrillard) or *recognition* (Augé), Virilio notes a complete *substitution* of the real.

Declaring that he finds the argument that seeks to distinguish between modernism and postmodernism entirely sterile, he situates himself first in the continuum of modernism that has neither resolution nor finality. John Armitage (2000) called this type of modernity a *hypermodernity*.

In this world, in mental and physical spheres of life, people are now controlled or, in greater likelihood, remotely controlled. As an example we can say that the street, a wellspring for the spatial story since the French Revolution of 1789, has lost its iconic status. Having lost the street in the nineteenth century the public is now, Virilio continues (in the depressive aftermath of 1968), losing the speech it had captured and so also its voice.[3] Deprived of existential territory and even of their right to speech, masses of people (a point that Etienne Balibar will develop in his work on citizenship) also witness the erosion of an effective degree of citizenship. The ever-stronger impact of electronic technologies that produce floating systems of value in all spheres of life has led Virilio to revise his earlier pronouncements. In another interview he asserts that humans now live in a truly postmodern age (Armitage 2011).

Writing at the Limit of a Tendency

Chronicling technological innovations and their impact on the subject living in the nation-state, the city and world-space, Virilio, like Baudrillard, claims to be writing at the "limit" of a tendency. As he puts it: "I try to reach the tendency" (Lotringer and Virilio 2008: 44). This "tendency" is what in their conjunction the capital and military sectors seek at once to disclose and to conceal. Most people live, he mocks in *The Information Bomb* (2000), much like nineteenth-century bourgeois, oblivious to the changes around them, while the rest of the population of the world-as-*banlieue* agonizes in poverty and violence. These accounts vary between muckraking journalism and science fiction. Like Baudrillard, who had a fascination for energy and circulation under flexible capitalism, Virilio adores and abhors what is wrought when controlling bodies take strategic command of technology. The critic's responsibility is to point to the loss of "human space" and, he hopes, to reintroduce some form of responsibility that would lead to a reinvention

---

3 Virilio develops this argument about the street in *Speed and Politics* (1986). He reminds readers how Haussman wanted to control the city and its inhabitants. Haussmann's map of Paris, "Nouveau Plan de Paris Fortifié" (1847), reprinted on the cover of the English translation, shows how the boulevards both encircle and cut up the city, thus facilitating the control of the milieu *and* of an unruly populace which was now prevented from taking to the street. Virilio also discusses the banishment of people, especially workers, to the *banlieue* outside of the old city limits, that is, of the new boulevards that act as a powerful barrier. The loss of voice is also central to Deleuze's argument in "Postscript on the Societies of Control" in *Negotiations* (1995).

of more existential or ecological spaces and the experience of "human time." The stumbling block is set at the border between humanism and science. The latter is no longer based on truth, which for the Enlightenment had been equated with justice, but only on research valued for its performative virtue. Modern science is a "techno-science" whose philosophical foundations have lost the light that inspired them. In industrial nations, research, he argues, is by and large directed toward the militarization of science. It is a trend that has to be accounted for both philosophically *and* ecologically. Scientific inquiry has lost the intellectual and critical rigor that had been born with its art of dispassionate observation. Today it is only a technological adventurism, much like extreme sports, which seeks to exceed itself.

Through advances in electronic engineering, science has accelerated the shift from a representation of the world (the world of mirrors and glasses) to one of presentation (the virtual world of electronic images conveyed through fiber optics). In the Renaissance, the gallery of mirrors introduced a major change in the domain of self-perception, whereas today humans witness such changes when, with the advent of the computer screen, virtual space replaces the reflective surface of the mirror, which had formerly been the guarantee of self-identity. From a world based on optical representation, humans have moved into a virtual counterpart that causes a total eclipse of the existential apprehension of the world. This marks a passage from an aesthetics based on appearance and being to one of disappearance, what Virilio calls an *esthétique de la disparition* (1980) that begins with photography and film and now includes digital technology. As a result of a shift in priorities based on commercial and logistical models of means and ends, a scientist no longer discovers truth by way of movement between experiment and experience. The savant is a champion, a star in a postmodern floating system of value devised by the media and a new social order. Alluding to the passing of the more heroic age of Descartes, Huygens, Newton and Leibniz, Virilio concludes that the evolution of scientific inquiry is part of a nihilism at the basis of a cybernetic era in which inquiry for the sake of inquiry has been eclipsed by stardom in a system based on signs and abstraction. This nihilism profoundly affects both subjectivity and society (Armitage 2001: 14). Such would be the "limit" of the tendency to invest truth in scientific inquiry under ideological control.

Human Bodies in Speed Space

Where in this dystopia can we find a geography of the body? Today, Virilio asserts, we speak of an energized body, not one of "bilateral symmetry," but rather one equipped with reflexes of anticipatory or premonitory disposition (Armitage 2000: 62). In a certain way the body becomes what it is because it is motorized. Energy, vitality and movement define the body, which is no longer a sculpted shape fashioned to be contemplated. Echoing and going beyond the fantasies of designers of perpetual-motion machines or even the automata of the Enlightenment, Virilio asserts that the human body as we knew it is becoming superfluous and expendable.

Humans, the critic reiterates, function best in extensive space and in existential time. Administrative and military orders have caused them to live at two speeds at once. One is in the matrix of an antiquated reality of everyday life and the other under the imperative of speed. One reality is based on diurnal and nocturnal activities, and the other on velocity. In the former people continue to live in extensive time when they represent themselves and their doings through the stories they tell, the memories they share, the archives they build and the writing (like Virilio's, which is compulsively copious) they publish in articles and books. When they deal with the intensive time of new technologies and with electronic time, the human being dissipates. The brain continues to belong to average time while electronic time belongs to robotic machines in a growing field of artificial intelligence now shown superseding human capacities for thought and action.

The consequences for humans, Virilio warns, are dire. The organic or existential spaces of psychic depth are at risk but, moreover, the "humanness" of humanity is lost. An almost paranoid vision—the kind of paranoia that Freud had called essential for the discovery of knowledge—leads Virilio to imagine that those in power manipulate information so as to create a kind of pseudo-individualism that cleverly hides the fact that those at the top of the new "social pyramid" go fast and reap all the benefits, while those at the base move at slower speeds. They are made to consume and have no real agency or velocity of their own. The vast majority of humans, however, do not have access even to this pyramid—or even to any kind of everyday life. They are parked in a global *banlieue* of sorts, in collective anomie. A globally networked society in which the electronic elite is perched on the summit is destined (in the fatalistic sense of the term) to fashion depthless human beings who live in the very solitude that Marc Augé finds in the contemporary human condition. Virilio is adamant that human subjects cannot simply be separated from their spatial context. If they are, they lose their sense of responsibility (Armitage 2000: 42). Virilio warns his readers that the Cold War, whose end signified not so much the triumph of liberalism as the failure of a type of social experimentation, has been replaced by a global economic war based on speed.

Far from producing "better" subjects and citizens, technology is shown simply invading them and imposing different sets of problems. Virilio sees market strategies producing the illusion of individual agency: to buttress his argument, he quotes Withold Gombrowicz as saying that a culture that has become inorganic reflects an immature or even larval state of being; inorganic culture appeals to humans who wrongly think that it liberates them from the "messiness" of everyday reality. The reader senses here the presence of the nightmarish underside of modernism and futurism, a world in which humans live within what elsewhere Virilio calls a strategy of deception in which a military and economic power elite is sanctioned to oppress and manipulate. Here and elsewhere his persistent use of literary and critical sources has the strategic value of favoring writing and duration (such as the printed book in which pronouncements are made) over the image and simultaneity (for example, podcasts and twitters, which are not Virilio's medium of choice).[4] He ratifies Freud who declared that writers have an especially keen sense of the world, indeed one of existential depth whose loss he so deplores (Virilio 1999). To open (mental) passages, a dimension that has disappeared in a digital world of skills and problem solving, the classical writers in Virilio's pantheon appeal to duration and reflection and not to instant reflexive response.[5]

As it is practiced today technology cannot embrace any form of humanism. Continuing where Augé left off, Virilio claims that formerly humans had relations (which defined space) and a past (which brought a sense of time to life as it was lived), but now they are overtaken by an acceleration of history to the point where they live entirely beyond the *hinc et nunc* so that, today, it can be said that "here begins elsewhere" (Virilio 2005a). It was the Cold War, he concurs with Baudrillard, that maintained an elegant balance of terror through a canny politics of fear

---

4   This is the argument that is made explicitly in *The Art of the Motor* (1995) for its premonition of the image replacing writing and of the cyberbody, wired to electronic objects, replacing the biological body.

5   On this point see Hélène Cixous (1998), who explicitly writes about resisting this tendency. She practices—and calls for—an *écrire-penser*, a *writing-thinking*, that is, one with a continuous opening of passages.

which spawned the techno-scientific explosion, including the invention of the internet. He is adamant that politics, moving from the military–industrial complex to its informational variant, is completely disconnected from everyday life. Yet a nagging question remains: what can be done when political struggles—women's rights, gay rights, post-colonial or ecological struggles and more—lag behind the post-industrial revolution and the techno-sciences? In the mode of the former Second World War worker-priests, *prêtres-ouvriers*, in the line of Emmanuel Mounier who committed their energies to the modest betterment of those lacking the necessities of life, Virilio declares (perhaps with false modesty) that he is completely out of phase with fashionable and glaringly visible political movements. He works with the homeless and with migrants, with people outside of the new social pyramid whose lives are at risk under the forces of globalization.[6]

The critics' task is double: they have to dispel the illusions in which the people in the lower half of the pyramid are shackled and help those who live in anomie. They also have to retrain sensibilities and revalorize activities that focus on those who are at the bottom or at the margins, such as social services and others who strive for the betterment of the planet and who currently are, from the point of view of the new elite, of little or no importance.

The Nation-State

In the last decades we have witnessed how the electronic revolution has transformed subjectivity. In a famous aside in *Mal d'archive* Jacques Derrida (1995: 33) fancied that, had Freud lived in the age of e-mail, psychoanalysis would never have seen the light of day. The implication is that the alteration of subjectivity has yielded new social hierarchies and *redistributed* (in the idiolect of Jacques Rancière) guiding spatial practices. One such involves the diminishing importance of the nation-state, which had been a webbing or matrix of social process. In the early writings that had been close to the ferment of 1968 Virilio joined other French intellectuals to decry abuses of state power. Where citizens had lost considerable agency under the dictates of the state, today, in the regime

---

6 Virilio acknowledges having worked with the Abbé Pierre. Other worker-priests in addition to Emmanuel Mounier included Michel de Certeau and Gilbert Cesbron. The latter's book about young homeless adolescents, provocatively entitled *Chiens perdus sans collier*, was made into a film by the same name and scandalized bourgeois readers and viewers of the 1950s.

of globalization, they lose even more. When the nation-state loses power citizens witness the erosion of the rights and privileges that had been guiding principles of the Revolution of 1789. Though not an adept of the "nation-state" and thinking more in terms of world citizenship, Virilio does not enjoy the current form of transnationalism that, dictated by the market, is further dissolving citizens' rights.

Virilio's vision of history confirms the point. Internationalism had marked the era of communism, but today geopolitics have largely disappeared in the face of global capitalism in which one market transacts international exchange at breakneck speed. Instantaneity is not the reality of distance or that of geographic intervention which once organized the nation-states. Tele-transmissions spell the alteration of extensive geography by producing a virtual reality. Today what is local is *outside* of the global sphere. It belongs to the periphery, to an intercontinentally impoverished *banlieue* often rent and torn by violence (Virilio 2005a). What is localized does not belong to the new social pyramid since it is *in situ*. With a portmanteau adjective Virilio declares that a *globalitarian* mutation is taking place. Localities are extroverted, turned inside out. The very places of livelihood are transported elsewhere when people are not. In the flexible regime they either follow or they are eliminated.

Delocalization not only affects the character of the individual but also indicates that nation-states—as well as real cities—are disappearing. To illustrate this point, Virilio argues that during his presidency Bill Clinton declared that the United States did not distinguish between domestic and foreign policy. The outside was the inside. Those who were truly outside and who resisted the global order had to be eliminated. In this respect the global city, connected to others of similar magnitude and density, replaces the nation-state of the nineteenth and twentieth centuries. When they are "wired" as they are, the cities of the entire world, he speculates, are telepresent to one another "24/7." Virilio becomes truly visionary in declaring that the "great optical transhorizon" results from the economic and political strategy of virtualization that makes globalization possible (Virilio 2005a). In the twenty-first century, there is pure communication or the unfolding of a media-space that covers the entire earth.

City-States and Citizens

If the nation-state is becoming history, what happens to the city or whatever complex that may be superseding it? Cities (Virilio prudently cites Paris rather than Los Angeles) are territorial concentrations. Like many older metropolises, Paris was born in extensive space. Since Ancient Greece—the return to Western origins signals that Virilio remains of classically European and French orientation—both the city and the state have been territorial phenomena to which citizens belonged by "right." The citizen (Virilio does not dwell on exclusions) was first a soldier who owned the right to a territory and a duty to defend it. The city today, as an effect of migration, demographic increases, accelerated intercontinental transportation and now the information revolution, has been replaced by a kind of megalopolis, a global sprawl, a space without center or periphery.[7] Real cities first turned into "overexposed cities" before becoming today's deterritorialized megacities which concentrate all the world's riches (2005a: 20). They are the center of financial transactions and direct the market economy. The real *polis* vanishes while we witness the advent of the new and unforeseen wasteland of an "unreal city."

With the dropping of the information bomb and the implementation of a general strategy of deception, what Virilio calls a redistributed emotional democracy replaces a political democracy. Since the attack on the World Trade Center in Manhattan and the consequent resurgence of terrorism, a kind of panic is instigated, exploited and maintained in these meta-cities with the goal of controlling their population. Virilio quotes American actress Susan Sarandon as saying that after the attacks of 9/11, politicians and the media have taken our emotions hostage. Humans are all blinded to the fact that terrorism has become endemic to a global world that has lost all borders separating inside from outside. The critics must shift attention from the subject's loss of symbolic and existential territories to the citizen's manipulation through the media. The fear that spreads through cities is based less on mental than instrumental images.

The new panic city is in the grip of terrorizing images. The creation of fear and dread derives from a carefully imposed synchronization of collective emotions to the degree that millions of inhabitants of a city are programmed to feel the same sensation at the same time (2005a). In this regime, urban centers, once sites of political action, have become cores of disaster. Not only are they the target of the most efficacious application of terrorism but they are also policed so as to produce uneven economic development. The old urban reality was based on space and time, while today's is in the new time of electronic transmission in which humans are present only by means of programming. To counter these

---

7 Here Virilio doubles Edward Soja (1989 and 1996) on what the latter calls, after Lefebvre and Foucault, the "spatial turn" of the last millennium. The entire world is undergoing an urbanization that will become its permanent condition.

effects Virilio advocates a geopolitics, a material politics showing that transmission and negotiations are not merely calibrated according to the speed of light. Ideas and mentalities cannot be put under the sign of "fair value." He reminds his fellow Frenchmen that the thread of the history of France

> lies buried beneath the density of metropolitan infrastructures that have, it would seem, freed man from the irregular surface of the ground: lifts, escalators of all description, dirigible balloons, aeroplanes, helicopters, supersonic jets and stratospheric rockets… all instruments of a progressive loss of the geopolitics of our origins in favor of a metropolitics that is fundamentally crepuscular. (Virilio 2005a: 16)

The world, Virilio concludes, is not only liberal; it is a teratological territory. When globalization abolishes both territory and rights, when elsewhere is here, the post-Nietzchean twilight of place, a *crépuscule des lieux*, is all that remains (2005a: 113–43).[8] Cybernetic space is but an *ersatz*, a substitution of reality for a reality without gravity. Virilio leaves his readers with the hardly reassuring conclusion that humans are adrift on the narrow blue planet whose great ecliptic band has become a *banlieue insalubre*, an insanitary ring that the sun traces around its circumference.

Politics and Culture

Over the years Virilio has shown how revolutions in transportation and information alter our relations to the world. In doing so he reaches deep into a romantic poetic imagination. The railway, as Alfred de Vigny observed at the end of his epic (and mostly forgotten) poem, "La maison du berger," allows city dwellers to reach a dwelling, the "habitus" of a thatched cottage or *chaumière*, at the price of polluting fumes belching from the smokestack of the wood-burning locomotive. The masts of ships that in "L'Invitation au voyage" Baudelaire describes gently wavering in soft amber light bear the promise of travel to faraway places that, on second thoughts and in others of the writer's reflections, are zones of colonial squalor. When, with the creation of images, optical illusions and a world of propaganda, it is now possible to affix the same poster everywhere in the world at the same time, culture itself has become a service category, a product on sale for consumers. With a single market, fears Virilio, humans witness the appearance of a cultural hypermarket. Art

8 Virilio plays on the French title of Richard Wagner's opera *Twilight of the Gods*, *Le crépuscule des dieux*.

that depends on inscription in nature or in a terrain—as he put it in *Bunker Archeology*, quoting Hölderlin, "art is the gift to nature"—has disappeared. It has been absorbed by consumerism and by advertisement.

Taking note of the the ebb and flow of colonization and decolonization, and of staggering population increases in the midst of the information revolution, Virilio proceeds with some caution when he urges his readers to reinvent, rather than simply to "go back to," political man. But how? No answers are readily available. In the age of electronics and of the rapid transfer of information, instead of a loss of humanness, are we not rather witnessing, as both Baudrillard and Augé had it and as Friedrich Kittler also states in an interview with Virilio, how traditional politics and culture are losing power under the effect of speed?[9] Culture and politics, Kittler counters Virilio, are predicated on everyday speech and a formal human nervous system that are both slow. Neither speech nor nervous systems can be handled any more without preparing, assisting or assuming some electronic decision-making process. How does a philosopher, writer or politician react to this condition? With the progressive loss of extensive space, stories, memories, archives, writings—even if they still exist—are replaced by an intensive space of electronic transmission and culture. When humans are deprived of duration, stories, memory and archives survive as remainders.

The proximity of territorial continuity that humans have been said to know for centuries is invoked in order to be put in question. Telecommunication is thus shown to bring humans closer to others than to the territories where they happen to be. Phenomenologist that he is, Virilio continues to ponder the consequences for perception when geographical space loses its importance. In what he might call the days of bygone physical reality, humans, he argues (basing his claims on the idea of a vast continuity of a now-deceased oral culture), believed in performance through speech. However, with the calibration of the speed of light applied to human activities, chronology has become measured in terms of displacement and perception. Perception and information fuse, and as a consequence new wars organize the space of society by means of competing assaults on the control of information. Global society lives in what the author calls real time, that is, the time in which information interacts in the context of electronic enterprise and bureaucracy. Humans can hardly dream at this point of a just and equilibrated society. They are divided into the camps of those who understand the consequences of actions taken in real time and those who do not. The information

9 Friedrich Kittler expands on the point in an interview with Virilio (Armitage 2001: 97–109).

network produces worldwide conglomerates that are no longer "multi-nationals" in the sense we knew in the 1970s. At no point does Virilio speculate how one could learn to look at space or at a networked world differently. Far from liberating humans, computer-assisted subjectivities are seen as eradicating agency. In the twentieth century, Turing and Wiener, the fathers of cybernetics, asked for controls to be imposed on computer systems. However, Virilio argues, they were still "free" intellectuals, neither "slaves" nor enjoined members of academies of knowledge as are the "specialists" of today who find themselves caught in an anonymous power system that is no longer identified with any state apparatus. Today, heroism is replaced by superstardom in a world without the real, where no one truly obtains agency or even shoulders responsibility. New forms of colonization and violence come with the ostensive liberation and circulation of information for the simple reason that critical thinking—such as what elsewhere Jacques Rancière (2004) calls *dissensus*—is discouraged in the interest of commercial enterprise. The decline of politics and culture is linked to that of writing. Writing has given way to a new and highly incontinent orality—where blogging has replaced storytelling—and an invasion of everyday life by the space of the image. Thus readers today, whose parents would have been the walkers and poachers in the world of Michel de Certeau, confront difficulty by forming mental images based on words. It is once again Friedrich Kittler who reminds Virilio that some natural phenomena cannot be entirely computerized for the simple reason that nature is not a computer. Similarly, some highly complex human phenomena fall outside of processing paradigms. Without them human space can be discerned only as corridors in circuits (Armitage 2001: 106). We cannot simply deplore the end of humankind but have to stress that culture and politics as they were known in the post-Second World War era up to the 1960s are no more.

The Future of the Planet

For Virilio power (in the mould of Foucault) is concealed yet obviously and evidently ubiquitous. As the green world shrinks the future of the planet does not shine bright under the rays of enlightened subjectivity. Constrained time and abstract space (which count among Lefebvre's watchwords) are signs of Virilio's "premonition" of imminent catastrophe. Democracies in the form of large urban centers are under the symbolic control of transnational entities in collusion with docile governments and the media. They transform people into *emotional* rather than *political* citizens by creating an atmosphere of panic by way of propaganda in order to dismantle collectively critical action. While formless, sprawling megacities are replete with riches, the *banlieues*, be they large centers or entire countries, are living in dire poverty. Bucking the trend that would have perceived the world to be networked or flat, Virilio asks his readers to look at the pyramidal shape of a transformed reality. He invents the idea of a past time of greater spiritual and ecological plenitude to call our attention to the sordid conditions of the present. Like Lefebvre, he astutely observes that some populations are so destitute that they cannot obtain consciousness of everyday reality. Existential dimensions bearing long-held categories of time and space may indeed be lost or, for that matter, may have never been. What counts, however, is to imagine how other existential territories can be formed in a world *assisted*, but not controlled, by technologies of speed. Focusing primarily on loss, no doubt by reason of his own messianic views, Virilio refuses to aim his energies in that direction. How can place be altered productively so that an existential relation with it does not entirely disappear under the force of acceleration? What can be done in an era that focuses primarily on economic performance and no longer on collective well-being? Virilio does not go beyond his wake-up call to "the sleepy nineteenth-century bourgeois" he sees around him. He wants to take his readers into the twenty-first century and point out to them the inventions and consequences of military and informational technologies.

This chapter began where Virilio and Augé seemingly concur in their views of the space of supermodernity. The wry ethnologist, writing about the contemporary condition of things, our "dream-wars," the ruins of time or the Parisian metro of times past and present locates spatial transformation where, in Virilio's words, social ties, *liens*, give way to places, *lieux*, of solitude. He distinguishes between the electrical world and the brave new world of electronics in which the speed of light robs humans of their habitable places—which include culture and politics—with extensive time and space. Arguing for sedentariness and going nowhere, as one critic puts it, in the face of blinding light (Redhead 2004: 160), Virilio expresses regret and cautions to a degree so extreme that we are left wondering what indeed is the future of our planet. Virilio leaves no doubt as to his grim vision of the future and humans' second postmodern condition:

> Today, we can also see that accelerated transportations and telecommunications force the world to operate under instantaneous conditions that nevertheless *have a real impact* on geography, history and on our sense of

real time and real space. But much more than the end of geography is at stake as the pollution of distances and substances takes hold. For the instantaneity of acceleration also signals the end of history, not in the sense that Francis Fukuyama argued, but in the sense that we have come to the end of the natural historical and spatial scale of earthly things, such as a human-centered sense of distance. As the former enormity of the world is reduced to nothing more than speed-space, then, geopolitics, geo-strategy, the human spatial scale of the city and the nation-state are accordingly obliterated in favor of the realm of the urban instant, a realm that is not simply far removed from the physical geography of the real world, but that is also the province of technologized traceability and contemporary trajectography of, in other words, an almost uninhabitable planet. (Armitage, 2009: 110–11)

It is not by chance that among Virilio's keenest readers are other dominant figures of the 1960s and beyond, notably Gilles Deleuze and Félix Guattari. Although they are dead and gone today their presence is vibrant and vivacious. That they conjugate a spatial aesthetic with political and philosophical agendas in frequent harmony with Virilio is hardly surprising.

6

Deleuze and Guattari: Space and Becoming

> If you believe in the world you precipitate events, however inconspicuous, that elude control, you engender new space-times, however small their surface or volume.
>
> Deleuze, *Negotiations*

Paul Virilio shows how the explosion of the information bomb has direct repercussions on humans and their experience of the nation-state, of the city and of world-space. Gilles Deleuze and Félix Guattari draw repeatedly on Virilio when they declare that every critical relation, no matter what discipline it uses or represents, has to be treated in view of the world he describes. As Virilio put it, when addressing what he calls Deleuze and Guattari's "poetic or nomadological understanding of the world,"

> [t]oday's world no longer has any kind of stability; it is shifting, like the polar ice-cap, or "continental drift". Nomadology is thus an idea which is in total accordance with what I feel with regard to speed and deterritorialization. So, it is hardly surprising that we clearly agree on the theme of deterritorialization. (Virilio 2005a: 40)

Spatial consciousness is ubiquitous in Deleuze and Guattari's writings. It informs their theory of an *event*, which Virilio employs in a catastrophic sense, insofar as a sensation of space often becomes the event as it "takes place" and is as quickly abolished.[1] It also subtends their politics, which in their lexicon means creating openings that will enable *becomings*. Becomings engage what so far has been called existential territorialization.

Extensive and Intensive Space

Written in the aftermath of the events of May 1968, *Anti-Oedipus*, the first volume of *Capitalism and Schizophrenia*, was a spirited attack on

---

1 The point is made in *L'Epuisé* (Deleuze 1992: 72–75). An event is a simultaneous objectivation and subjectivation of the world, a "nexus" of perceptions and of "prehensions" that the individual experiences in his or her heightened awareness of locale and of totality.

capitalism, the state and tributary institutions that included the family, school, religion and, especially, psychiatry.[2] It argued that the contemporary world finds its subjects imprisoned in spaces that are at once stratified and striated, everywhere riddled and cut through by locative coordinates that plot the ways that the world can be thought of. Under the cloak of normalcy in the sphere of capitalism humans are molded into obedient subjects whose docility upholds the social order into which they are born. The "state" and its economic machinery employ what the authors call *order-words* ("mots d'ordre") to define the character of communication and commerce, which administrate obedience and docility. Order-words tell their receivers what they must do, how they must behave and where and how they must consume.

While *Anti-Oedipus* is a rampant critique of capitalism and the state's barbaric hold on civilization, the sequel, *A Thousand Plateaus* (1980) writes of novel ways of thinking that lead to new processes of subjectivation and of "becoming" that have as a common point of departure the types of spatial practice that Michel de Certeau had put forward. Inventive ways of crafting time and space are shown to be modes of creative resistance. The book (of epic proportion) is aimed against the state apparatus that Deleuze and Guattari see ratifying existing values while disciplining thinking and bodily behavior. They want to invent ways of philosophizing otherwise, according to a "bastard" line. They do not so much oppose metaphysics as re-read philosophers from the pre-Socratics to Spinoza, and from Hume to Nietzsche, a corpus that the post-Napoleonic pedagogy of philosophy had excluded from national curricula, possibly by reason of their Jewish, English, German or other foreign origins. *A Thousand Plateaus* reads as a patchwork of emblems, of images intersecting with texts, that implicitly argue (by way of suggestive gaps and overlappings of words and pictures) that history is a mosaic and that the idea of a *telos* has to be replaced by Nietzschean becoming. The very title of the book is rich in spatial implications: plateaus are components of a stratigraphy of the world and its millennial age in which time as duration cannot be accorded a chronology that humans can comprehend. Borrowed from the British anthropologist, Gregory Bateson, plateau owes its definition to Balinese culture: a plateau or plane of consistency is marked by an intensity, making possible a certain composition that is held together in space and time. A plateau, they

2 In an interview with Catherine Clément, Gilles Deleuze states: "May was for Félix and me an event. Even though we did not know each other at the time, it can be said that *Anti-Oedipus* is written as a result of 68" (Backès-Clément 1995).

declare, is a network of lines having no clear borders dividing an inside from an outside. It has no beginning or end, only a *milieu*, that is, in French, both a median and an environment. It does not follow the Western model of a climax as a point of arrest. It reaches a threshold at which it metamorphoses into a different composition altogether.

Once the intensity of a plateau dissipates, it leaves after-images that can be reactivated anywhere and any time. Certain readers (as the authors suggest when they compare their work to a toolbox whose contents enable a process of becoming) will draw a special dynamism from some of the plateaus and use them in their own lives for purposes of resistance and affirmation. Several plateaus deal more explicitly with space, from the rhizome to smooth space, nomadic space and territory in relation to processes of subjectivation, to the city, to the state as well as to capitalist places, and even to the utterings and echoes of order-words. Their "after-images" from other times and places gain importance in a post-68 world wherever worldwide resistance to capitalism and colonial policy is being revived. From Algeria to Vietnam, from Cuba to Civil Rights and the Black Panthers in the United States, resistance movements spring up quasi-spontaneously anywhere, but always against the *state* and its colonizing powers. To resist creatively, the opening of new spaces fosters the mobilization of other ways of thinking within and outside of given orders.

The concept of space as a site of practice makes possible what Deleuze and Guattari call the creation of new "processes of subjectivation." Along another axis, from *A Thousand Plateaus* to Guattari's *Three Ecologies* and Deleuze's writings on politics in *Negotiations*, a slight shift in the treatment of space is discerned at the point where the philosophers move from a criticism of the disciplinary society to a criticism of one, like Virilio's "information complex," defined by rapid economic globalization. With the waning of the state the philosopher and the psychoanalyst note the renewed importance of the cities where the world's populations are concentrated, which now are sites under the dictates of transnational commerce that *homogenize* subjects so as to make them eat, sleep and think along programmed lines. In *The Anti-Oedipus* the authors had reflected on the oedipal nature of the uni-dimensional mode of life emblematized by the extraordinary slogan—so simple, yet so telling—*métro, boulot, dodo* (subway, job, sleep). Almost a decade later they see the dehumanizing and ecologically disastrous effects accruing with logarithmic progression under the impact of a marketing empire governed by a new elite. "Marketing," Deleuze writes, "is now the instrument of social control and produces the arrogant breed who are our masters" (1995: 181).

Lines and Vectors

That is why in *A Thousand Plateaus* Deleuze and Guattari acknowledge time and again their debt to Bateson who, in *Steps to an Ecology of Mind*, a handbook in the anti-war movement in the United States at the time of its publication (as a popular and cheap paperback), wrote against the concept of the individual—a capitalist invention—and argued that humans cannot be separated from their environment. The anthropologist used the plus sign to connect, to make bonds that are at once *liens* (links) and its anagram, *lines*: human + human + environment = an ecology of mind. Going even further, Deleuze and Guattari write that the world—which includes humans but without being anthropocentric—is composed of lines, segments and articulations of segments. Lines, be they of latitude or longitude, neither begin nor end. Active in essence, they detach themselves from a mental or physical territory. They deterritorialize while simultaneously, forming new territories and strata, they reterritorialize. At times they become lines of flight that lead to new compositions altogether.

Here Deleuze and Guattari build on Virilio's concept of velocity. While they do not deviate from his conjecture that "speed" in the West is a form of war in collusion first with industrial production and later with information, they engage its different velocities and have it move along a variety of vectors. Speed is a component of desire because it causes desire to be a function of movement. Motion, emotion: desire is marked by acceleration and deceleration, now by rapid flow and then by pause, anticipation and re-engagement. Speed informs psychoanalysis (Freud ponders the unsettling image of himself in "The Uncanny" when he is in a moving train) and philosophy (a science built on the errant motion of its cynics and pre-Socratics). As many philosophers and scientists from Heraclitus to complexity theorists have argued, the world is in perpetual motion. Deleuze and Guattari infer that the modes of state reason that underpin the disciplinary society tend to "fixate," that is, to locate and to pigeonhole the multilateral, ever-moving and always creative potential of *thinking*, an activity that resists imposing orders of control.

For Deleuze and Guattari space is sensed intensively rather than extensively. In their thumbnail history of the impact and after-effects of international capitalism, they compare different uses of space in what, in 1980, they see as the hemispheres of the East and the West. Though neither part of the world gains privilege over the other, they give a slight nod to the East. It is less in the territorial, rooted West than in the intermediate areas especially in the East that rhizomatic thinking is manifest: on steppes, deserts, plains and grasslands where adventitious plants spread about and over surfaces of hard soil or shifting sands and rocks. In "Rhizome," a piece that serves as an introduction to *A Thousand Plateaus*, the philosophers urge their readers to think adventurously and adventitiously, to replace binary thought (even that which generates the opposition of a root to the rhizome), which is based on "either/or," with an "and" or "+", that is, with new ways of thinking and of making alliances. The latter include an ethos and a style, or a manner of living in the world and of holding things together. Consisting of lines, not of points or positions, such as the root of a carrot, turnip, parsnip or a tree, rhizomes are made solely of connections instead of inclusions and exclusions. They are grasses and filaments, or even the system of shallow mycelia. Light, flexible and horizontal, they move between points, creating thousands of interstices and pattern networks without borders. Taken in a general sense, beyond the world of botany from which the figure is borrowed, rhizomes are defined by a circulations of states of things and intensities related to sexes, animals, vegetables, the world, politics, books and things at once natural and artificial. As Deleuze and Guattari put it, included are "all manners of becoming."

Because the opposition is heuristic, a single term cannot be entirely dissociated from the others. A tree grows not only in Brooklyn but also within every human. Trees, whose rings make clear the presence of a singular or collective "elephantine" memory (it suffices to recall the moment in *Vertigo*, one of Deleuze's favorite films, when Scottie [James Stewart] peers at the concentric rings of the stump of a giant sequoia), would be of a long-term variety, while their counterpart might be the mycelium of a mushroom that grows (if it is mycorrhizal) in a parasitical relation with the tree's roots. The mushroom remembers to sprout when conditions are favorable, and it forgets about the task of fruiting when they are not. Short-term memory is induced by writing and by the making of maps. Quoting Jean-Luc Godard, Deleuze and Guattari assert: "Don't have a just idea, just have an idea:" pry open micro-spaces, not macro-spaces. Long-term memory is institutional, archival and selectively collective among social classes that are said to be stable and ensconced in their strata. Rhizomatic offshoots, the philosophers claim, connect on a plane of consistency. They construct assemblages that cannot be associated with Rand-McNally, Michelin or Google Earth. Along this line, to write is to resist, to make an alternative map, and to make such a map is to make a rhizome. To map is to traverse spaces in a process of continual deterritorializing and reterritorializing. To write is not to represent a finite, a pre-established and a pre-existing world, but to survey and plot worlds to come.

Rather than being marked by metric units, rhizomes are discerned only as *varieties of measurement* or multiplicities. Units or unities are always related to a power or an order that imposes a force of subjectivation. Rhizomes are anti-genealogical. They free subjects from their "Oedipal prison" in which everyone is supposed to "do time" in a disciplinary society. They undo vertical or hierarchical patterns of state thought. Rhizomatic multiplicities are defined by their outside, that is, by an abstract line of deterritorialization and, at the limit, by a line of flight along which any point can and must be connected to something else. With the advent of the rhizome comes that of a mode of apprehension of intensities and of *haecceities*, or surface compositions without embedded foundations. The *haecceity* can be likened to what Alois Riegl long ago called a haptic process of reading the world "all over," in every which direction, without succumbing to the centering or centripetal force of identification. Rhizomes, *haecceities* and multiplicities move along surfaces without being confined to a *Grund* or foundation, much as Heathcliff and Cathy, the main protagonists of *Wuthering Heights*. Space, strictly speaking, is opened between lines.

Smooth Spaces

To rhizomatic thinking, Deleuze and Guattari add the concept of smooth space, which has its counterpart in striation. Smooth space opens to the tracing of lines, diagrams, to movement and nomadic thought (1987: ch. 12). The philosopher and the psychoanalyst introduce smooth space to inaugurate and develop the concept of nomadism and the war machine. Taking up the after-image of the nomads of the thirteenth century on the steppes of Asia, they assume the Mongolian plateau to be the antithesis of the built, propertied environment of the West and praise nomads for the way they occupy space and for inventing the war machine to embattle the centralized, "rooted" state. It is made abundantly clear that nomadic mobility, errancy or wandering do not rely only on physical movement. The vagabond quality of true nomads, they claim, is marked by the fact that they can move without moving and without imitation of the movement of others. Nomadism is the motivating force of those who assemble or "occupy" a place temporarily and then move on. The ground of the nomad, if a ground there is, is in the "molecular" (and not "molar") order they embody. Their ground is *smooth* rather than being laced with borders that confine their activities or plot them in a gridded configuration. Smooth space is not to be traversed. It makes possible "becomings" (drawn from *le devenir*, an infinitive substantive). By strong contrast, striated space consists of points, parallels, horizontal and vertical stratifications and diagonals. It is organizational (and molar), in other words of an aggregate and agglomerated, often compressed, quality. Extending their line of inquiry, Deleuze and Guattari argue that striated spaces—though existing since time immemorial—were found abundantly in the disciplinary society of the nineteenth century but also in the current condition of finance capitalism. As in the opposition of the rhizome to the root, the two types of space are present in and about each other. Lines will always separate from even the most striated of spaces—such as today's cities—to begin forming new smooth surfaces in the mental maps of the inhabitants.

Already in *A Thousand Plateaus*, twelve years after the events of May 1968, the authors observe the effects of the intensification of global capitalism. They are keenly aware of the growing power of the military–industrial–informational complex and the rise of transnational markets. Again acknowledging a debt to Virilio, they show how what became the military–industrial complex (a term coined by Dwight Eisenhower after 1954, at the height of the Cold War) appropriated the nomadic war machine and created its own smooth spaces on the sea and in the air:

> As Virilio emphasizes, the sea became the place of the *fleet in being*, where one no longer goes from one point to another, but rather holds space beginning from any point: instead of striating space, one occupies it with a vector of deterritorialization in perpetual motion. This modern strategy was communicated from the sea to the air, as the new smooth space, but also to the entire Earth considered as desert or sea. As converter and capturer, the State does not just relativize movement, it reimparts absolute movement. It does not just go from the smooth to the striated, it reconstitutes smooth space; it reimparts smooth in the wake of the striated. It is true that this new nomadism accompanies a worldwide war machine whose organization exceeds the State apparatuses and passes into energy, military-industrial, and multinational complexes. (Deleuze and Guattari 1987: 386–87)

They underscore that smooth space is not just revolutionary, in the utopian conviction of 1968, but that the nomadic process itself can be captured by capitalist forces. The nomadic war machine aimed at state power that appeared on the Asian steppes of the thirteenth century and that they find again in the 1960s can also, as they are keenly aware, be co-opted by capitalist strategies.

Since they died in 1992 (Guattari) and 1995 (Deleuze), the psychoanalyst and the philosopher were never able to consider smooth spaces created by information and new media, which Virilio severely criticizes in *The Information Bomb* (1998), *Strategies of Deception* (1999) and even more so in *City of Panic* (2004), on the state of the city in a post 9/11 world. Yet in their earlier engagements, contrary to Virilio, Deleuze and (especially) Guattari, while cautioning against the reappropriation of the binary digit by information science (Deleuze and Guattari 1987: 5), are committed to the development of computer-assisted subjectivities as a means to combat the disciplinary order of state-thought. While they were prescient about new media in the 1980s, they never witnessed the impact it has had over the past decade and a half. Their arguments for opening of spaces that allow maximal circulation are engaged in an ongoing struggle against the state apparatuses and their worldwide war machines of France, Europe, the United States and, at the time, the Soviet Union. In *A Thousand Plateaus*, the state owns two poles of sovereignty, that of *imperium* with its summit and that of the republic of free spirits with its *extensio*. The two are in constant interference but are also necessary to each other. In 1980 Deleuze and Guattari still hope that an event will occur in passing from one to the other that will be outside the state's all-encompassing thought-images, which permeate all human endeavor. The event (it was not to be the fall of the Berlin Wall) is whatever enables the opening of spaces as a condition for other ways of thinking. By way of Foucault, Deleuze and Guattari argue that humans are about to leave this type of society. With the rise of military–industrial capitalism, the state and its institutions lose power.

Along with the weakening of the bureaucratic state Deleuze and Guattari foresee the growing importance of the city as the site of a problematic relationship with the nation-state that would no longer be its container. City and state have always found themselves at odds with each other. Tracing the history of the rivalry and discussing the growing importance of the city at the expense of the state in the second half of the twentieth century, they conclude that the city becomes the striated space par excellence, what Virilio will call the city-state. They oppose *nomos*, the open, non-partitioned space, to *polis*, the city as it is experienced and negotiated by its inhabitants, transients and citizens. The earth is open space, a surface that agriculture begins to striate in conjunction with the development of the town. Since the Greeks the city has continued this process of stratification. However, the striated city always gives rise to new smooth spaces, to the degree that on our urbanized planet there are sites where other, or new, smooth "pockets" continue to make resistance possible.

Strong emphasis is placed on either resisting or cutting through the institutions, lineages and genealogies that had marked the striations of the state. Inert and immobile, state space imposes all kinds of immutable and monumental forms that are generally vertical and hierarchical. Readers are urged to resist this strategic model through rhizomatic and nomadic modes of thinking. An ongoing movement of deterritorializing and reterritorializing is vital, they continue, for opening new spaces that destratify and recompose the segmented patterns of space brought about by disciplinary orders.

In the wake of 1968 and other simultaneous uprisings all over the world, Deleuze and Guattari had hoped briefly for a generalized "becoming-minoritarian." In a sweeping polemical flourish, the authors assert that this can displace or even dethrone the majoritarian body of which the white, working, male city-dweller of thirty-five years is an emblem. Minorities are entities found in any and every social structure who can put dominant thought and its order-words in question (Deleuze and Guattari state repeatedly) to precipitate events, to create interruptions, to dilate our ways of thinking, to "open passages" and to bring forth new compositions and other ways of inventing. They coin the metaphor of the tribe that resists the state: tribes, nomads and the inhabitants of shanty towns possess tactical mobility and a capacity for realizing smooth space. This romantic and utopian view of the capacity of the *favela*, the *banlieue* and the nebulous zone of squalor and human disenchantment to become minoritarian is not based on numbers (which would foment mass upheaval) but on relations to the number. A majority striates space and measures time where it makes use of "numbered numbers" (*nombres nombrés*) while a minority puts striated space in question by the construction of new lines. It has recourse to "numbering numbers" (*nombres nombrants*). It redistributes a place in order to have it *become space*. It recomposes and traces angles, curves and lines that deviate from parallel lines. Majority and minority are not predicated on numbers but on ways of occupying space. Segmented space, which is under the sign of *chronos*, of measured time, is contrasted with smooth space distributed under the sign of *aeon*, that is, time of duration or time without chronology. The language of the minoritarian deviates by introducing differences into the official or majoritarian language.

Erewhon *Now Here*

Almost thirty years after its publication the romantic tone of *A Thousand Plateaus* seems nostalgic and, at the same time, vitally utopian. The tone anticipates the moment in *What is Philosophy?*, published eleven years later, where the two authors are quick to pick up the obvious point that Samuel Butler's *Erewhon* is a sort of "verlan" for *Nowhere*. But they add that the author wanted to describe the non-place also as *now here*, a state of virtual force and action, which cannot be located or restricted to a zone of non-being. Nonetheless, in 1991 the events of 1968 that inspired a good part of the utopian tenor of the work are but a distant memory. The worldwide resistance glimpsed in the 1960s did not change the world for the better. In 1989 the fall of the Berlin Wall and, shortly after, the apparent collapse of the Soviet Union ushered in new forms of capitalism and transnational powers so strong that they threatened to signal the demise of any and all utopian activity.

In *The Three Ecologies,* one of his last texts (written in 1989), which might be considered a sequel to *A Thousand Plateaus*, Félix Guattari addresses problems of ecological space and subjectivation in relation to globalization in a post-communist world. He adapts his concepts to a new context in which the degradation of the world as well as the absence of a correlation between human or social development and technological achievements are manifest. Again invoking Virilio to draw awareness to the plight of humans yoked to consumerist technologies, Guattari stresses the need to use analytical tools to address the conditions of global markets and Virilio's megacities. However, against all the odds, he continues to believe in the possibility of creating openings even in the most minutely striated spaces. Guattari seeks to shatter a homogenized, media-dominated subjectivity and to decenter Western values based on profit motives. In the words of Rancière, he seeks to think (from) a locus that is not simply connected to economics (Rancière 2009). He appeals to a need to look to other cultures in order to find alternatives to the norms from which the Western subject derives a sense of identity. Guattari remains vague about what he calls the media. He primarily calls television into question, but not technologies that enable the making of new connections. Because of the media, he claims, subjects have no way of calling for change. They do not have wider access to their desire nor can they, in the midst of its blare, hear a voice of their own timbre. In a surprising turn for readers of *Anti-Oedipus* and *A Thousand Plateaus*, Guattari declares that a "subject" is needed that will open spaces and lead to changes both in micro- *and* in macro-politics. Minoritarians have to militate for rights and immigrants for new contracts of citizenship. For this, a collective militancy—a new *macro-politics* of sorts—is necessary. If Guattari insists more on militancy than in the 1970s when desire was the watchword for liberation, he avoids the return of simple oppositions.

Militancy, he insists, can only be temporary. Humans have to be "analytically militant." They have to think and act and must always become singular again. They need *micro-politics* that are part of an "*ecosophy*"—a wisdom of managing one's *oikos* or house in the widest sense—scaffolded upon aesthetic and ethical paradigms.

In 1989, in a "post-communist" world, capitalism appeared as triumphant—if we were to believe the media—and the East–West antagonism of the Cold War seemed to have been replaced by a still largely unknown multi-polar world. The time is right, Guattari writes, to address the North–South axis along which the injustices of capitalism abound. He underlines the fact that not only terror (in Virilio's sense) but poverty is *endemic* to capitalism. The arguments are difficult to refute: new ways of thinking and other social relations are the pre-conditions for any change to follow in natural ecology; an ecosophy that *includes* the earth is needed; ecology, or the study of the law of the *oikos*, of the habitat, cannot be given over to folkloristic movements that want to go "back to the earth." We have to think *how* to live on this earth, how to make it habitable for human projects for as long as it lasts, in a globally urbanized world-space in which acceleration, mutation and substantial demographic increases are the order of things (Virilio 2005a). In line with a practical strain of utopian thought, it is imperative to think the future from the present. What Guattari then perceived to be an ecological crisis on a global scale—one that has quintupled over the past two decades—cannot be given only to technocrats for resolution. Changes in thinking are a prerequisite for solving problems of energy, water or air. What Guattari will call the new "eco-logy" or logic of intensity that he proposes is predicated on an included middle. It deals with mental circulation, with the creation of spaces where new affects can take hold, where new sensibilities and other forms of intelligence develop. Only on this kind of surface will human relations with nature ever change.

The bureaucratic state, Guattari notes, has lost much of its mettle. However, its diminishment did not open fissures or apertures. A new global elite has since laminated social differences and conflicts inherited from the Hegelian and Marxian views of the social complex. Nation-states are obsolete because a new *imperium*, that of the global market, which is vastly different from the old *sovereign imperium* discussed in *A Thousand Plateaus*, has perfected its capture of smooth space and now dictates the order of the state. Guattari had shown earlier how capitalism is not made of infra- and superstructure but of undifferentiated flows or, in a newer idiolect, streams. The market constructs a plane of equivalence between material assets, cultural assets and nature itself. In this respect both domestic and international relations are increasingly under the yoke of military machineries: local wars have become ubiquitous and have yielded immense profit for the techno-scientific and transnational establishments that found and develop them. Guattari sees the collusive media increasingly imposing the model of one-world culture. They infantilize the subjects by administering mental sedatives. Class antagonisms have given way to bipolar and multi-polar fields of subjectivity; social, economic and international contexts have become increasingly "complexified" to the extent that change is difficult to envisage. The working-class subjectivity, which in classical Marxism was the carrier of consciousness and the voice of the future, has been overtaken by the advent of consumer society in lockstep with the media. Though they are *lived* intensely, class divisions have become smokescreens that cause the decision-making power of the new dominant class to be less immediately perceptible than that of its bourgeois predecessor. Class divisions have been replaced by a vague sense of social or cultural belonging that can easily be manipulated, as in another context Jacques Rancière, in his *Haine de la démocratie* (2005), has made clear in his definition of a post-democratic culture ruled by "consensus."

Reconstructing the Subject

In an era in which 1968 is a vanishing illusion, Guattari declares that "*le sujet ne va pas de soi*," the subject is not a straightforward matter (2000: 35). It has to be reconstructed and held away from the media, which have cannibalized subjectivity under a veil of equality and sameness. To construct a "subject" for this new world-space, Guattari nonetheless revisits his former pronouncements. The "subject" deviates from a territory with the assistance of diagrams and plotted lines. He or she does not have an Oedipal relation with his or her masters or parents. The subject (who can be both one and many) deterritorializes softly in order to avert an abrupt deterritorialization that might easily lead to implosion or castigation. The subject continually deterritorializes and reterritorializes by opening spaces to make possible the construction of new territories and compositions. If Virilio claims ownership of the term deterritorialization, it is Guattari who amplifies it and modifies its use. Where Virilio warned of a generalized deterritorialization under the imperative of speed, Guattari urges the construction of concretely mental territories tied to life instead of death (the money of the media). Along the way are jettisoned a good number of scientific pronouncements, including those of psychoanalysis, that produce false constants of normality, induce identities and prevent invention. Without abandoning Freudian paradigms Guattari retains the concept of the unconscious which, he asserts, is not pre-structural or fixated on the past but open to the future. It operates partially at a pre-personal level and is open to change. As such the subject is "autopoietic," performative, welcoming and connecting with alterity. It is even open to mutations.

Tellingly, especially from the hypotheses that grounds every chapter of this study, in order to argue for the construction of existential territories, Guattari mobilizes the Sartrean concepts of *en-soi*, a fixed and rigid *in-itself*, and *pour-soi*, a fragile but enabling subject that is open to the outside and never identical to itself. Like Sartre, he finds grist for his mill more in the domain of aesthetics and literature—Beckett, Kafka, Proust—than in medical science. Guattari's new subject must have continued mobility in thinking so as to prevent *rigor mortis* or striation at either the singular or collective level. Resistance to presently striated spaces and molar subjects comes often from the arts, be it literature, music, architecture, cinema or painting. It is plugged into micro-politics. Even the smallest event, Guattari believes, can produce changes of the magnitude of Bateson's celebrated butterfly whose flapping wings on one side of the globe bear on the state of things on the other.

A New Sense of Responsibility

In the post-communist world what Guattari calls "Integrated World Capitalism" spans the globe and leaves swathes of misery and ecological havoc with the advent of "flows." He sees them "streaming" from capitalism founded upon four quasi-interchangeable semiotic regimes—economic, juridical, scientific and, ultimately, another that pertains to subjectivation. The latter region becomes the point of departure for the realization of utopian ideas. It is where *nowhere* is *now here*. Taking off from Virilio's statements about superstardom and a concomitant intellectual loss of responsibility, Guattari appeals indirectly to Sartre by declaring that all those who deal with the construction of subjectivity—artists of various kinds, teachers, architects, people in sports or fashion—must get out of their transferential neutrality. They have the responsibility of helping reconstruct the subject as a way of either being outside or of resisting these new forms of capitalism. Micro-spaces have to be opened in the onslaught of communication and information. Of a piece with Certeau and Augé, Guattari quotes Walter Benjamin who contrasts communication with the art of storytelling:

> Storytelling ... does not aim to convey the pure essence of a thing, like information or a report. It sinks the thing into the life of the storyteller, in order to bring it out of him again. Thus traces of the storyteller clings to the story the way the handprints of the potter cling to the clay vessel. (2000: 67)

The analogy requires some "unpacking": communication is exactly what good literature does *not* do well; the storyteller communicates obliquely and slyly in order to make the site of the performance become the space of meaning. Unfettered communication, while vital and necessary, lacks the quality of an event that comes with the performance of the tale. Literature thus theorizes communication through its own modes of obfuscation. It is incumbent upon us to watch out for "pseudo-stories"—and designer-art—that are solely the product of the market. In the regime of electronic capitalism, Guattari reminds us, creations are co-opted as soon as they are invented. Guattari reasserts the importance of continuous creativity as a form of micro-politics, an art of making "precious little" things possible. Creative resistance can be singular and collective, aesthetic and ethical, always at odds with media-generated pseudo-stories and false consumer art that can be recognized by its "vitaminic function" (1995: 132).

Given the magnitude of global capitalism, resistance becomes a difficult art of both the objects and the milieus of everyday life. Guattari finishes with another utopian flourish in coining *ecosophy*, a philosophy-of-the-world, at once applied and theoretical, ethico-political and aesthetic, that necessarily would have to *move away from the old forms* of political, religious and associative commitment. With painful memories of the French communist intellectuals' blind allegiance to the Stalinist party-line in the post-war era, Guattari is adamant that political action, hardly a simple renewal of the earlier opiating effects of 'militancy', will be a multifaceted movement, deploying agencies (*instances*) and mechanisms "that will simultaneously *analyze* and *produce* subjectivities" (1989: 68, my emphasis). Theory and practice will coalesce in order to recreate the world through the three lenses of mental, social and natural ecology, in ongoing processes of deterritorialization and reterritorialization. Mental ecology, in which a maximum of circulation occurs in a smooth space, depends on aesthetic invention. For social ecology, a new ethics, that is, new relations to one's own body and to others, have to be conceived. Natural ecology will thrive on subjects reinventing the world with technologies aimed toward living things rather than toward destructive conflict.

Since 1968, the administrative spaces of the state have given way to more heavily striated world-spaces that include the new megacities that are the centers of "Integrated World Capitalism." Guattari sees that, within what he calls the "global struggle," minoritarian groups operate transversally. Ecology—the point is capital—affects the world both locally and globally by cutting across all struggles. The making habitable of the world is not equated with a deep structure or a new religion, but with a highly effective element for alternative *subjectivation* (a recon-struction of the subject) and for the dynamics of ecological territories. In 1989, with the rise of fundamentalism and a civil war in Algeria, Guattari saw Muslims engaged in "internal struggles" that were out of synch with global efforts being made elsewhere to make the world more habitable. He considered fundamentalist quarrels as a passing phase in a world that was, he hoped, about to re-create itself *ecosophically*. Almost two decades later, Guattari's predictions have had less "premonitory" value than what Augé predicted or what Virilio states about the impact of the information complex. The Cold War and even the "post-communist" world are now points of debate more than hard facts of reality. Since 2001 the resurgence of terrorism would seem to have voided Guattari's predictions, or at least further complicated issues in ways he could not foretell. Yet the ecological relation he holds with space cannot be ques-tioned. It remains a point of reference for ethical and political agendas of our time.

After Control

It is also Gilles Deleuze's belief that salutary changes in our world come directly from a creative social body rather than from the political sphere. However, the last section of *Negotiations*, entitled "Politics" (two inter-views published in French in 1990 and 1991), deals with the changes that have occurred in the midst of the evolution from a disciplinary society to one of control. In using the term "society of control" (which he borrows from William Burroughs) Deleuze recognizes that transnational markets and global cities have supplanted the idea of the state. The emphasis on worldwide marketing has reduced the number of assemblages or possible compositions among differently "dissenting" subjects. At the same time, the subject as individual with a signature has been reclaimed to be a "dividual" with an access code; crowds have become "samples." The world is more than ever made up of people competing against one another in the flexible era of expanded capital. In 1968 Michel de Certeau held a belief in the possibility of capturing speech, of obtaining the right to put into performance words heretofore unknown. For Deleuze, in the 1990s, this possibility of thinking of speech is chimerical. Without nostalgia, he notes that

> speech has gone to hell; it is rotten to the core. No one, no group, can capture speech any more. Speech has been taken over by information and communication. Even art has been taken up into the art market. When everything is under the spell of marketing, art can no longer serve as a locus of resistance. There exists no voice that is not immediately recuperated. (1995: 176)

Deleuze's first interviewer, Antonio Negri, notes that, in later works, notably *Foucault* (1986) and *The Fold* (1988), the philosopher seems to give more attention to processes of subjectivation than in *A Thousand Plateaus*. He would seem to follow the same path as Guattari. In global world-space the subject resisting state power has disappeared under the onslaught of media. Deleuze does not elaborate. He simply restates a faith in social action, affirming that collective creativity can never be entirely sanctioned or shunted into opiate living. What, in the wake of Bergson, Deleuze calls "fabulation" rather than fiction, the power of imaginative vision, is needed to invent new spaces from which to think otherwise. Deleuze stakes his claims on older works of literature, music and painting, citing examples from Mallarmé, Rimbaud, Klee, Berg, the Straubs and Garrel (Deleuze 1995: 174). Uncannily echoing Certeau in *The Practice of Everyday Life*, he asks that with these artists people pry open *vacuoles* or interruptors within the sphere of control. As an afterthought, and in the mode of a worker-priest or a convert to a renewed mode of existentialism, he laments that humans no longer believe in the world:

> What we most lack is a belief in the world, we've quite lost the world, it's been taken from us. If you believe in the world you precipitate events, however inconspicuous, that elude control, you engender new space-times, however small their surface or volume. It's what you call pietas. (1995: 176)

This is what he elsewhere calls "grace": against those who practice irony, cynicism or dismissive nostalgia Deleuze declares that we must commit ourselves to the world as a locus of affirmation, and we must believe in social action as a resource for change.

Rearranging Theories

A number of questions remain in the wake of Deleuze and Guattari's reflections inaugurated after 1968. What happens to subjects when the state loses power? How do new media transform processes of subjectivation? How do humans negotiate new problems of mental and physical borders connected to large numbers of legal and illegal immigrants? What happens to the fact of becoming minoritarian in a world-space when people are more and more caught in a regime of numbered numbers, of measured and linear time (*chronos*) and when, in a world dominated by economics and the market, minorities also seek to become majorities? What kind of ecological micro-spaces is it still possible to open when the world has become, according to Paul Virilio, a planetary suburb?

The beginning of an answer can be found in what Guattari already noted in *Molecular Revolution*: our theoretical tools have to be constantly adjusted and recalibrated:

> There is no example anywhere in the sciences of this sort of respect for the texts and formulae propounded by the giants [Marx and Freud] of the past. Revisionism is the norm. We are endlessly relativizing, rearranging, dismantling all the accepted theories, and those that resist remain under permanent attack. Far from setting out to mummify them, the aim is to open them out onto further constructions that are just as provisional but more firmly grounded in the solid earth of experience. What matters, in the last resort, is how a theory is used. (Guattari 1984: 253)

A theory is what invents or implements an opening, a capture of space. Now, to locate that capture in a world with waning nation-states and striated city-states, it is worthwhile to turn to Bruno Latour and to Etienne Balibar.

7

Bruno Latour: Common Spaces

We must not save vanishing existential spaces but ask how we can exist in a networked world.
> Latour, *Paris: ville invisible* (my translation)

Coexistence begins in space more than in time.
> Latour, *Paris: ville invisible*

A common space emerges only through discussion and negotiations.
> Latour, *War of the Worlds*

There is probably no more decisive difference among thinkers than the position they are inclined to take on space: Is space that within which objects and subjects reside? Or is space one of the many connections made by objects and subjects?
> Latour, "Spheres and Networks"

The writers studied up to now have all been suspicious of the idea that technology will bring salvation to our current spatial crises. They concur, too, when they champion an existential relation with place and space in order to mitigate the damages of unfettered capitalism and modernism. Bruno Latour follows their path. Trained both as a philosopher and an anthropologist, he emphatically declares that all over the world technological developments have altered our grasp of space and time as well as that of the nature and quality of subjectivity. They have repercussions on city- and world-spaces. However, Latour criticizes those who declare that machines dominate us from the top down. He rejects the fiction of a society living in the yoke of a highly circumscribed power elite. He asks how it is possible to live in a world whose demographic density has increased enormously and where space is lacking. How, under these conditions, can humans make the world habitable? It is imperative, he writes, to bring to the fore some of the ways humans can collaborate and create a common space in a rapidly transforming urban mosaic.

A type of machine is operative as a metaphor for every age: the windmill and catapult were the crowning mechanical perfection of the Middle Ages; the cannon, harquebus and ocean-going vessel in the Renaissance; the pullies operating dams, dykes, and sluices of canals in the classical age; the guillotine and chronometer in the Enlightenment; the steam engine in the nineteenth century. Our age is represented by computers, especially the figure of networks through which humans have chosen to represent themselves. With this metaphor, divisions between inside and outside are collapsed; the center is replaced by a large number of temporary knots and fragile threads along which humans and things ceaselessly circulate. We must take into account the techno-scientific achievements without which humans could not live in our world, Latour argues, and we also need to rethink modernity not only as an era of invention and development but as the seedbed of some reductive concepts, namely, of nature and culture versus reason, technology and science.[1] We must look toward a *non-modernism* in which our inherited spatial coordinates can be rethought and reconfigured.

Machinic networks are vital to the construction of new milieus. Far from leading humans into abstraction as they had for existential humanists, they reconnect us with the real and with what Latour calls "the concrete" which makes possible our lives in contemporary cities and the world, which now consists of myriad, at times intersecting, networks that connect and reconnect humans and machines in continuous transformation. We live and think in cascades of words and images existing only through figuration, which he understands to be a process of alignment, referencing and formatting. A sentence or a mouse-click will apparently arrest their circulation and literally reduce them to a cliché.[2] Such an arrest, for Latour, is an illusion or a fiction of sorts. *Ego, hic et nunc* (the self, here and now): fictions all, the individual, place and time are the result of alignments and interpretations of events. Like the ego, Latour claims, society exists only as a result of multifarious alignments and of what is made of them. The individual is a *furet* in the game of that name, the "slipper" or hidden object, helped by mediators, that circulates along mobile networks, in constant movement and transformation.[3] Relayed by a proliferation of mediators, we now move and act *in* these networks and not *on* a system. These hypotheses are demonstrated concretely

1   See "Why has Critique Run Out of Steam? From Matters of Fact to Matters of Concern" (2004: 225–48) in which Latour upbraids the very readers of the journal, *Critical Inquiry*, in which his words are published for not having updated their thinking.

2   The etymology of cliché reaches back to *clicher*, an onomatopoeia, from the sound of a typographical matrix hitting molten metal before it fuses. It reputedly originated during the French Revolution, during the heyday of the ephemeral pamphlet and *mazarinade*. It is thus related to *cliquer*, to impress.

3   *Furet* is a ferret, an animal known to be constantly searching and circulating. It has given its name to a game—pass the slipper—in which a thing, the *furet*, is rapidly circulated among participants while one person has to guess who has it. Latour coins the term *actor-network theory*. Actors (*actants*) do not act on a structure but circulate along threads in networks (Latour 1999, 2005).

where space is theorized in a text written for a book-catalog and web project, *Paris: ville invisible* (1998), which was part of an exhibition and for which photographs were provided by Emilie Hermant.

Alignments, traversals, formatting

A fiction of modernism, and an artifact of the nineteenth century, the panoptic view and the panorama—such as the one offered to spectators from the roof of the now-defunct department store, La Samaritaine— give way to perspectives obtained on computer screens often located underground. On them we can see small-scale panoramas that render traceable and almost palpable the everyday fabrication of a "'plasma' in which we are all immersed" (Latour and Hermant 1998: 13). They might be called "oligoptics," though these are always ephemeral and never control society from the top down as had been the case in the fictions of modernism that still have currency for many theorists of culture. Latour rejects widely held fears that the computer could lead to social fragmentation or a collective homogenization. Those who assert that the last traces of a vanishing world are found in the cafés and small shops on the winding streets of quaint French villages are out of date. Vanishing existential spaces are not to be saved but to be seen in the context of humans managing urban- and world-spaces as best they can. Humans have to learn to exist in networks. Much depends on a chosen point of view (1998: 14). Latour proposes a series of photographs of the city aligned in order to be read in continuous fashion, without isolation of any from the others. What we call the social or its figure, Latour argues, will become visible when we manage to link together all the particular traces that traverse it at ultra-high velocity. "These traces, trajectories, meanderings, these partial illuminations, these phosphorescences make Paris, the City of Light, sparkle. Paris, the invisible city, is made of them" (1998: 14). Referring indirectly to Calvino's *Invisible Cities*, Latour argues that "invisible" does not refer to some memory trace or spiritual element but to a very *concrete* trace that contemporary machines and mediators leave on their users. Simple circuits and pathways replace "beautiful images," and theory, now understood as procession, supersedes picturesque narrative.[4] A written text such as his own, he claims, has no other goal than

4 His reference is to Jean Baudrillard's "precession of simulacra." Latour wants to revalorize a slightly different meaning of the word theory—today understood as contemplation—that once meant a *procession* to consult an oracle. In his lexicon it is a putting into movement and a traversal.

to introduce a *tension* into graphic documents that in turn have no other *intention* than to traverse or go about the city of Paris shown from a certain angle and followed along certain lines by way of many mediating vehicles (1998: 14). A social theory suitable to our moment should bring people closer to the cities in which they live.

When we move from a graphic document and a bureaucratic inscription to a geographic medium our itinerary does not proceed from the social milieu to places outside of its ambit. In today's "second world," for Latour, the displacement has simply become a change in medium, in institution, in graphs or in scale. In a networked world, to "circulate" or to "situate" begins concretely. In a city such as Paris streets have to be given names, inscribed in registers and thus made visible on computer screens. Written traces have to be turned into legible signs (*pancartes*). Humans constantly shuttle back and forth between the concrete and another medium, often that of the computer.

If, Latour notes, we begin by following the figuration of a social milieu that is in ongoing movement, we find only offices, hallways, instruments, files, alignments and teams, never anything that can be totalized under the name of "society." We in fact never find any synchronization of the *individual* with *society* (1998: 36). In addition to signboards, humans have to learn to follow the *bordereaux*, lists or detailed memoranda that enumerate all the hidden elements that underlie information. Such would be the list that leads from an espresso that a client orders at the Café de Flore (a jibe at Sartre and his transcendental philosophical musings) to the outrageous price it commands, or from delight at the sight of apricots on display at the market in Rungis to the discourse of economics that reveals how they were transported to Paris from Chile. Humans do not live in *information societies* but in *societies in ongoing transformation* in which data are always in a condition of transfer.

In an oblique critique of Baudrillard, Latour takes up the Borgesian truism that "the map is not the territory." This proverb, like any cliché worth its salt, ought to prevent humans from falling into the trap of megalomania or of paranoia: megalomaniacs confuse the map and the territory because they think they can dominate the space before their eyes, while the paranoid believe that they are dominated by and under the surveillance of someone hidden in a small, secret space somewhere at the end of an electronic cable wired to a room filled with television monitors. They both mistake for pure "information" what in reality is but a *cascade* of "transformations." To produce a figure of the social, we need to learn to replace simple *transfers of information* with ongoing *transformations* that are always concrete.

Writing against a trend in French thought that takes a cautious view of images as reflections or even as dubious substitutions for reality, Latour argues that it is wrong to be suspicious of an image or to say that an image refers us only to an absent structure of society (Latour and Weibel 2002). The visible does not reside either in one image alone or in something outside of that image. In the second world in which we live the image exists only as a montage and in a *cheminement*, a routing, a traversal of sorts, less through nature—as in the first world—than along an ever-bifurcating pathway through different photographic angles. Images give form and introduce relations. Phenomena as such do not *appear in* the image. They too become visible only through what is being transformed, transported and deformed from one image to the next. Images are linked by a trace that enables humans to come and go, to circulate along a path both laterally and transversally. In order to see and to make a reference, we must follow the movement or perceptions of this trace through all the gaps and hiatuses of its transformation. Only by following such a trace will it again become possible to produce a figuration (*figure*) of the social and of the world that surrounds us, the very world, Latour wryly adds, that modernism had tried so hard to eradicate.

Following the lead of Jack Goody (1977), Latour claims that "while becoming more complicated, organizations that produce a city like Paris are actually being simplified—hence the proliferation of computer screens visible everywhere, whether we deal with the weather, nerves, a classroom, streets or with living beings" (1998: 53). The expression "information society" (or Virilio's analogue of the "information complex") has meaning only, he adds, if we refer to the increasing materialization in bauds and bits of what until now was thought in metaphysical terms to be part of an "ungraspable spirit" of social life. The more information we have, the more we can detect what links humans together, since cables, forms, modems, bouquets and platforms are becoming more visible. Because of these listings, every relation expresses fully what heretofore was thought to be much too complex. We cannot simply put aside all the bureaucratic adjustments and transformations by means of lenses, objectives, spreadsheets, files, institutions, data banks, that is, all the minuscule places where totalities are created. The dimensions we are contemplating do not come from the size of the images but from the connections they establish and their speed (*rapidité*) of circulation.

From subjects to generic beings

The same holds true for the individual subject. Latour revives Lévi-Strauss's distinction between hot and cold societies when he engages with the theme that seems to obsess the post-1968 philosophers of space: that a brave new world is causing an existential relation with time and matter to disappear, and that the vanishing is due to economic and technological acceleration or "heat." In a cold society, Latour acknowledges, the individual exists. He or she is firmly embedded in kinship structures, in symbolic networks, places and anthropological spaces. In a hot society individuals resemble targets toward which a series of missiles and missives are directed. Latour employs sagittal metaphors to describe this new individual who is studded by arrows of love, insect bites, fits of jealousy, bedbugs, viral attacks, narcissistic wounds and the sudden fire of passion that flushes the cheeks. An individual with a name "camps" at the unstable intersection of all these vectors, vehicles or angles of attack that help him or her to live or die. These vectors make up all the vibrations that compose what is wrongly referred to as "subject" or even worse as "intersubjectivity." Similarly, a city-space is not composed of a general frame in which interactions between subject and object converge. Paris is at most a series of aggregates that never really constitute "a society." To get away from a modernist reduction and to have recourse to a new figure of the social or to the social as figuration is to do away with the "individual" *and* with "society." Like a pixel, each small part is of the same configuration as the whole. As soon as it is put in motion, the *furet* or slipper of the social traces novel paths and digs more actively than the mole of an earlier regime.[5] The individual never *appears* as such. He or she, as Latour explains elsewhere in his work on actor-network theory (Latour 1999), exists only as a result of mediation.

Far from leading humans to abstraction or domination, machines enable them to refigure the social milieu in ways that produce many "virtuals" and open spaces. Humans neither act on a system nor are they entrapped in a structure. They simply watch vehicles pass by. Their footprints bear the traces of a structure through which they have chosen to represent themselves. These vehicles, Latour predicts confidently, will soon overtake humans. Most social theories inhabit the "utopian world" of the zoom. Yet the belief in a totality—be it that of the sky or the

---

5 The metaphors of the *furet* and the mole relate to two different historical times. Earlier, *la taupe*, the mole, was said to dig under ground and subvert. Today, the *furet* moves along networks in a flat world, undoing hierarchies more actively than the mole, a figure that had been dear to Marx.

market—that would include all others is an illusion or a fiction. An ego or "I" does not simply walk *through* the city in the manner of Certeau's practitioners of everyday life. The "I" consists of different forms of action and regimes of intelligence with no relation between them. The chosen examples are revealing. The "I" has wherewithal enough to be part of the following scenario:

> When I withdraw money from an automatic teller, I behave like a generic being with an individual code; pushing against the control barrier in the subway, I become a mechanical force that is pushing against another. In front of a set of traffic lights, I become a reader of signs capable of under-standing what is prohibited. Yelling at a bad driver, I become an indignant moral citizen; walking down the rue Saint-André-des-Arts, I join without thinking about it the natural flow (*flot*) of pilgrims; reading a book by Rouleau, I shift toward the discipline of philosophy to meditate on the silent influence of hidden forms. From one second to the next, different regimes of action relay each other to make me proceed from one competence to another. I am neither at the control nor am I without control. I am formatted. (1998: 101)

The "I" who is "I" by reason of the *choses* or commodities he or she owns *chooses* myriad possibilities of existence that are part of the devices located all over the city. The self that needs to go from one assignation to the next is not an individual or a force; he or she is not a marionette either but, rather, a thread that links these successive capsules of antici-pated selves that others have formatted. Like the rest of the social world, threads are woven, knotted, or move about much like mycelia or rhizomes. Urban spaces are covered with a multitude of formattings shaping generic beings of different forms, nature, consciousness and intentionalities who can all be summarized under the name of users or *usagers*. The "self" is a multitude of beings, a swarm of singularities. Myriad selves are everywhere, ubiquitous, sharing their habits and habitat with one and all. It is in the very folds of these "beings" that the "I" comes to lodge, the folds of a multiple body.

Criticizing those who argued for the necessity of a return to existen-tial ways of being or those who argue that we shuttle back and forth between familiar and other spaces, Latour asserts that humans are contin-ually bombarded by many possible existences which come to them by means of lights, flashes, shop windows and electronic publicity. Most humans participate in many networks at once while moving along their pathways and going from one to the next. It is not so much that they leave behind an existential territory as that they live in multiple networks which make up their existence. In the city, he claims (perhaps echoing Jean-Luc Godard's characters in the films shot in Paris in the 1960s), humans have the feeling of being overtaken by events. Most inhabitants or *agissants* (actors), however, are not human because objects simply carry out in time the function that was given to them. "The world is not constant as an essence but only through labor" (1998: 120).

Theorizing (in) Networks

If the social world is flat and the self is de facto distributed in space and time, then why, Latour asks, is it never discussed as something that is continuously being traced? Why is it always presented as the effect of a zoom, as a sphere or a pyramid? Today's panoptic views exist mainly as circulations of postcards, vignettes and verbal clichés. The latter endlessly compose and recompose the social world in various ways. Now that the world is "flat" they offer the collectivity, claims Latour, different possibilities for assembling and constructing common spaces. Without the fixity of social structures, theorists can no longer economize on the effort of working through figuration (or "scenarization"). Instead Latour proposes that they "subscribe" to different networks. The way people subscribe to electricity supplies and cable television—they are all *bons bourgeois*, all financially secure—indicates that they have freedom to subscribe to other networks, that is, to everything else that circulates in the city. In order to exist in today's second nature, human actors (*agissants*) must have myriad subscriptions. And so, in their daily interactions, much as in Perec's late writings about living in the city, they circulate in many networks at once, subscribing to psychology, economics, sociology and other disciplines. They can circulate along the trajectories of these figures but without stopping at a single image of any one of them. Likewise (as Latour reasons by analogy), the city is composed of many people who enter into a collectivity and create common spaces only with great difficulty.

Intellectuals and theorists wrongly think that their task is to strip away illusion, to impose "a critical distance," to "unveil appearances" and to make us aware of the forces of the market and various forms of media-manipulation. This type of criticism is based on the antiquated belief in a full reality or the post-Hegelian desire for totality. Instead, humans have to learn to follow the mediators while making mediation visible. Instead of obsessively unveiling the *real* hidden structures in order to find kernels of truth in our world, we can proceed by multiplying the mediators (possibly of the kind Certeau had identified in his sociology of communication [1997a: 117–23]). Such action would help drown the megalomaniacs and the paranoid in a rising tide of simple actors (*agis-*

sants). We are no longer part of a heroic age. Like computers, intellectuals (from Benjamin to Baudrillard) have been miniaturized and pocket-sized. Their stature is diminished and their books now come on small disks. Their pronouncements cannot aspire to totality, as they had in the heyday of Sartrean existentialism, in our own age of miniaturization and multiplicity.

It is unlikely, Latour emphasizes, that the social world today is composed of the same elements as a hundred years ago: that is, with the same individuals, crowds, mass movements, social classes, professions, norms, rules, cultures, structures, habits or laws. We need, he urges, is to hybridize a discipline such as sociology with others—with ethnology, economics or information. And just as we are multidisciplinary, so too we live in multifarious urban spaces, in the midst of crowds, masses *and* in different technologies. To see how humans live in great numbers in common urban spaces, we need to follow the multiple traces to the insignificant places where they form ephemeral tableaus composed of traces of streets, hallways, settings in Parisian cafés, or the verbal clichés such as "*Vive la France!*" heard in their midst. We have to see how mediators enable people to apprehend themselves partially and always provisionally as an array of things.

For Latour, humans can choose between two types of images of a city. On the one hand, a certain Paris, like the old bridge called the Pont Neuf, is real. The bridge is a kind of mineral frame from which powerless bodies, weighted down by a mass of clichés, must detach themselves. On the other, we can think of Paris as something virtual that, for the past two thousand years, has been renewing itself. To be able to invoke the real and the virtual Pont Neuf gives hope to the inhabitants of the city who will no longer suffocate in the narrow margins of freedom drawn by the theoretical determinations of an existential heritage.

Everything changes when it can be shown that all these "oligoptics" occupy only a few square feet, but their networks span the city—and the globe—by means of very thin, gossamer filaments that can snap at any time. Latour asks: What is in between? Nothing, except for space that enables humans to breath more freely. Time, which was essential for modernism, has been replaced by space whose fabrication is especially abundant in an age of networks. Paris is flat and the networks of surveillance barely scratch the city, which escapes them entirely. The word "power" no longer designates a state of things but a series of small displacements. The word "virtual" does not refer to some tele-unloading of the city on to the web that would indeed, writes Latour, be the ultimate form of disincarnation (1998: 166), but a return to true virtualities.

Power or *pouvoir* becomes potentiality and possibility. We live in a kind of dispersed plasma that seeks form. Like this plasma, power as *puissance*, as Michel Foucault had long ago argued, is invisible. Latour advocates another way of thinking, away from the modernist schema that still underlies many humanistic disciplines. Latour's examples (from the card-carrying self at the ATM to the customers in the Café Flore) are taken from an affluent city. Networks, however, though they might replace Virilio's seemingly more modernist form of a social pyramid, still create riches and poverty even if, instead of being ordered vertically, they are linked in a horizontal movement of perpetual transformation. Our suspicions of Latour in relation to his political stance are quelled when he becomes a harsh critic of modernist dreams, coupled with a direct politicization of networks. There we see how intimate and immediate locales of our own are folded with those of world-spaces.

Constructing Spaces in Common

Latour shows that electronic technologies transform the existential territories associated with Paris. His analysis of a specific city-space can be applied to others both in the West and elsewhere. He develops his constructivist argument in taking as his point of departure 9/11, an event that in the United States precipitated a sense of *emergency* (Latour 2002). What suddenly *emerged* in 2001 was the realization that a new world-space no longer follows that of the West and of modernism under the aegis of its civilizing and controlling mission for the rest of humanity. He has yet to explain how, in a world that is no longer unified, we might construct common spaces. Latour does not contrast the city with the nation-state. Rather, he extends his analyses from the city to what he somewhat vaguely refers to as "the West," which in 2001 is comprised of the European nations, the United States, Australia and Japan. It is both geopolitical and ideological. Blind to the changed world-space, this "West" continues to thrive on modernist concepts. It claims that science—a discipline many post-Cartesian spatial thinkers dismiss for introducing false, reductionist constants and for its dehumanizing tendency—is universal and given to truth. Without rejecting science *tout court* Latour shows how the current concept functions in a now-defunct context. Modernists established an untenable division between science and nature. They created a false multiplicity by putting nature on the side of human cultures. Just as a modernist perspective, in the manner of Le Corbusier, that had been deployed to dominate the city is now defunct, so also is that which wants to control the entire world under its naturalizing gaze. A colonizing and controlling gaze is replaced today by a very different, pressing issue: the urgent need to construct a common world-space.

The idea is further developed when a look around the world confirms that much of humanity has been bypassed by a belief in the vision of modernism. Although populations equipped with telecommunications and accelerated transportation are no longer locked into narrow confines and are "in touch" with the world, great masses of humanity have not found themselves unified. If humans "move" anywhere, it is toward a so-called "universal democracy" imposed by force on those who resist. "Unity" cannot happen with a mouse-click but has to be actively and patiently constructed. Latour urges his readers to recognize that humans are living in what he calls a "war of the worlds." The real question is: "how do we construct 'peace,' that is to say, a unified, common world-space?" (2002: 37). The current war, Latour declares, is not one between civilizations, as Samuel Huntington had it in *The Clash of Civilizations* (1997); rather, it is the result of the erroneous (modernist) belief in a universal Western science and reason. Until now a false peace reigned because the West and its scientists continued to believe in a universal nature that holds many cultures in its web. In a global world new kinds of negotiations are required to construct a common space. How? Latour does not want to have modern violence—in which Western reason covers the world—replaced by pre-modern violence. He wants to bring about new kinds of negotiations in a global world that still lives under the illusion of the dreams of modernism. Today, one's own world, that is, one's own *spatial fiction*, has to be negotiated *and* mediated with the world at large. To build a common world-space with co-existing networks humans are obliged to negotiate, to be not only technical but also human mediators.

Anthropologists, sociologists, cultural critics and artists recognize the existence of many cultural wars set against the backdrop of rational Western science. Reasoning from the point of view of modernists, they look upon other cultures with a tolerance that does not grant them an ontological status, and declare that these conflicts are always local. Their modernist world—in the singular—is that of science and technology, concepts that have been complemented by those of the market, democracy and even human rights. This world is ethnocentric, mainly American and, Latour writes, even "Yankee" (2002: 9). The process of unification is the self-proclaimed "responsibility," even the prerogative, of the West, which views itself as one culture having privilege over others. Countries of the Western alliance think of themselves as unique cultural groups that are part of a unifying modernity. Humanity, it is felt, has to enter into the harsh reality of science, technology and the market, which Latour sarcastically calls the new holy trinity.

Foreseeing the war in Iraq, he writes that contemporary wars are means by which the West pacifies conflicts by appealing to the idea of a single world. Though all people are fundamentally equal through trade, dominance and avoidance, Westerners, as defined above and without any particular ethnic appurtenance, put themselves at the center. When a nation such as the United States deals with the world at large it disregards its own ethnic or class differences and thinks of itself as a unified core. In a modernist, "majoritarian" framework of this sort cultures have no ontological status. When they are "comparable," traditional fields such as comparative anthropology or even comparative literature find new impetus. "We are the world" is for Latour the cliché (formerly a slogan Pepsi-Cola had crafted shortly after 1968) of a global nexus of Western scientists, engineers, economists and global democrats. To construct common singular and plural world-spaces, Latour insists that what in 2001 he calls multi-*culturalism* has to be complemented by a multi-*naturalism*. Today, the world, Latour declares provocatively, is less global than it had been in 1790, 1848, 1968 or even in 1989, when it was still possible to tie humanity to a Western idea of peaceful unity. The last two dates, we have seen, are important for many of the theorists of space discussed so far. The events of 1968 and their aftermath were hailed as "the dawn" for a new humanity (Lefebvre), a capture of speech (Certeau) and an opening for a generalized becoming-minoritarian (Deleuze and Guattari). Under the banner of a global social experiment the moment was one in which a reordering of space was countenanced. In 1989, the fall of the Soviet Union opened up a perceived unification through liberal and pan-democratic capitalism. For Latour, such globalizing visions are no longer possible after 2001.

The problem is—and Latour does well to point it out—that much of the West continues to function outside of a feedback loop. Diverse and multi-polar, composed of multiple networks, the world has to be actively pieced together by negotiation and mediation (2002: 30). Nobody can constitute the unity of the world for others as was the case in the eras of modernism and even postmodernism, by "offering to let others in" on condition that they abandon their existential sense of ontology. The outcome of this new war of the worlds is uncertain. Negotiations replace a simple belief in the ineluctable march of progress. After modernism and postmodernism we have arrived, Latour declares, at a second modernism or a "non-modernism" in which possibility amounts to multi-directional becomings.

Intellectual Diplomats

"We have to construct a common space" (2002: 37), Latour announces, and jettison rationalists and technocrats in favor of intellectual diplomats. The latter are not simply superior arbiters because they know how to argue with delicate urgency (or politely and with civility, as Etienne Balibar will argue) for common world-spaces. Natural laws allow one to judge cultural diversity. Construction, by contrast, means that facts too are fabricated (from fetishes to gods, values, works of art, politics, landscapes, nations). It is a new (and old) position in which *opposites* are recognized. It differs from modernism, which allowed no *oppositions* in its path of progress. Intellectual diplomats construct and experiment in a networked world in ongoing ways. The facts they discern are products of construction and fabrication, and as a consequence the question diplomats have to ask is not whether the fact or object is constructed but *how* and by what means. When only one truth is said to exist, the very notion of nature is conceived to oversee progressive agreement about the slow composition of a common world. As long as we *impose* Western notions of nature, science, economics and technology, we prevent a progressively crafted agreement to create a unified world-space.

Today, negotiations can begin only if all those concerned give up their own exoticisms and their perverse complacencies. We must distinguish (Latour echoes Certeau) between theories of universal rights and the practical means implementing them. Westerners have to negotiate while showing a *"constructivist face instead of a normalizing gaze"* (2002: 49, emphasis added). Latour's non-modernist constructivism functions positively. It asks questions. Does the free, rights-bearing individual have to be generalized to the whole world? Should we not rather add this conception as one in a series of possible persons, masks or identities? The non-modernist does not come on to the world's stage to put it in "order" but realizes that he or she is only one face, one mask in a play whose ending is uncertain.

Politics too have to be renegotiated. Under the inherited modern ideal a false sense of peace was based on the assumption that democracy, together with its principles of representation, cohesion and solidarity, is universal. Modernists, among whom Latour no doubt includes the leaders of industrial nations, cannot simply try to institute a "Western-style" democracy while asking others (whom they colonize in the sphere of democracy) to give up their institutions, their coordinates of space and time, their values and feelings (2002: 49). To build a non-modernist *cosmopolitics*, it must be universally recognized that as long as the West imposes its notions of nature and reason, negotiated agreements about world-space cannot be realized (Stengers 1996). Defining points (science, God, individualism, economics, politics) that had been taken as axioms need to be clarified and resolved in an ongoing effort to construct a common world in which *possibility* becomes a watchword. The modernist concept of actors acting on a system is replaced by one where negotiators circulate along networks that involve mediators—in other words, objects as well as people. A unified world-space can emerge at the intersection of these negotiations. Negotiators ask how to fabricate city- and world-spaces as well as new subjectivities. A "cosmopolitics" in the sense of Isabelle Stengers implies an active and ongoing construction of a common world-space.

Latour urges us to focus less on how to recover existential spaces than on how to exist in networks and how to live in common in an urban world increasingly populated by humans and machines. In the second nature in which we all live, subjectivity and the coordinates of time and space have drastically changed. Defending his notion of network, he recently wrote that:

> When we ponder how the global world could be made habitable [...] we now mean habitable for billions of humans and trillions of other creatures that no longer form a nature or, of course, a society, but rather, to use my term, a possible *collective* (contrary to the dual notions of nature-and-society, the collective is *not* collected yet, and no one has the slightest idea of what it is to be composed, how it is to be assembled, or even if it should be assembled into one piece). But why has the world been made uninhabitable in the first place? More precisely, why has it not been conceived as if the question of its habitability was the only question worth asking? (2009: 141, author's italics)

The answer lies, for him, in what he calls "*the lack of space.*" And he adds that "the whole enterprise around networks [which superficially] may look like a reduction, a limitation to many local scenes, is, in fact, a search for space, for a vastly more comfortably inhabitable space" (2009: 141). This search for ecological spaces that include artifice leads him to conclude (unlike Thomas Friedman) that even if a technologically connected world is flat, it is not unified. Latour urges intellectuals and theorists to take charge diplomatically in negotiations concerning the construction of common spaces. He wants to introduce the virtual and politics (in their Aristotelian sense as the art of the possible) into cities in order to create a true cosmopolitics. The latter would differ radically from a universal cosmopolitanism under the spell of the market. He advocates cultural translation for the sake of gaining understanding of the spatial fictions with which different cultures construct themselves. Latour is emphatic: all is construction—a statement that could, in turn, be seen as reductionist. Modernist power, such as that wielded by the United States and its allies, must be replaced by a true unification of different worlds in such a way that alliances are not based solely on economic status. While we can but wholeheartedly agree with Latour's somewhat romantic fictions about the creation of common spaces, it is difficult to see how underdeveloped countries or regions would be drawn into their negotiations. Similarly, we already noted that his formatted, city-dwelling selves tend to be affluent. Their status presupposes that they are already citizens possessing freedom of choice. What happens, we could ask, to those who fall outside of this category, to those who do not have the economic status to subscribe to networks? What can be asked about the city can also be asked about the nation-state and world-space. While buying into the idea of networks, the instability of a self in "hot" societies, the proliferation of mediators and, additionally, the necessity to negotiate, translate and decenter, do we not have to draw in geopolitics and citizenship to complement the subject? And even without imposing a psychoanalytical template, is there not a minimal kernel of a self, what used to be called "another scene"—be it singular or collective—that becomes precisely the locus of friction that creates resistance during negotiations? Even if the world is flat, in a post-2001 world of economic and electronic globalization, is geopolitics not still pertinent? Latour declares that to "re-engineer" their imaginations, architects, urban and "Earth" planners, social scientists, citizens and others cannot turn to the past but have to inhabit an entirely new place (2010: 127). Where, he ponders without answering, will they learn their new skills? Where and how will we indeed learn to inhabit this new planet Earth? With Lefebvre, Certeau, Augé and Deleuze and Guattari in mind, can we still think of existential territories that would account for the alterations of space that are taking place? For a theoretical and practical approach that has much in common with Latour we can turn to Etienne Balibar.

8

Etienne Balibar: Fictional Spaces

Intellectuals translate in order to help create a new space, then they efface themselves.

Balibar, *Droit de cité*

Etienne Balibar's name does not immediately come to mind as a spatial or ecological thinker. A student of Louis Althusser, Balibar was first known for his structural re-reading of Marx, especially for his contributions to *Reading "Capital"* (1965) in which he studied modes of production, reproduction and the reconstruction of social relations. The mode of analysis he employs in his work of the 1960s and 70s already "spatializes" the world through emphasis on social structures and practices. Since co-authoring with Immanuel Wallerstein a volume entitled *Race, Nation, Class* (1988), he has devoted much of his writing to problems of democracy in relation to globalization. He identifies two flows, a flow of transnational capital that sets a "trend" (of the kind Baudrillard and Virilio identify) and a massive flow of population. Both are the consequence of decolonization and now, especially, of globalization. Movements of population show him that we need to rethink what we mean by "space" on national, European and worldwide plateaus. He analyzes the relation that moves across subjects and citizens, and militates for an active rethinking of culture and politics at a time when decolonization, economic globalization and forced migration require affirmation of the grounding principles of Marx's political economy.

Balibar raises questions about borders, the construction of territories, the nation-state and the construction of global world-space. More than describing complete spaces, he focuses, in the wake of Marx, on the *articulation* of action on and across their plateaus. Balibar urges us, however much we mediate our relations with the world through technology, to think and act, *at once* individually and collectively, as subjects with agency and as active citizens. The subject has to be complemented by a citizen who is not merely the victim of marketing strategies, as we have seen in Baudrillard's economy of the sign. Less pessimistic than Virilio, Balibar does not exclude the possibility of such a citizen. For him, the concept of citizenship is tied to the rights of citizens on one level and, no less intimately, to those of "foreigners" on the other. All move and dwell in three geopolitical spaces of increasing scale: the French nation-state, the European Union and a world-space. The three must be considered, paradoxically, at once successively and simultaneously. Balibar argues against a modernist Western *universalism* (whose character resembles the modernism that Latour castigates), which he replaces with competing *universalities* that require ongoing mediation and negotiation.

The French Nation-State

Balibar sees the global world from a French context. Because of globalization, the constraints under which the French live today now extend far beyond the borders of their country. Money flows and changing technologies notwithstanding, internal problems arise "where cultures overlap, where the old and the new, the near and the far, collide" (1998: 6).[1] France can no longer be considered as a self-enclosed territory. At the heart of geopolitics, questions of democracy and citizenship are not deduced from abstract or theoretical formulations. Their very articulation is dictated by the constraints of a conjuncture in space (geography) and in time (history). However, the current conditions of a country such as France, built as it is on its own, often exceptionalist traditions, lend to it a particular profile with specific dilemmas. Balibar continues to champion the intellectual whose responsibility in a media-driven world is to formulate what he calls *burning* questions of the moment and, thus, to resist the influence of those who use "wrong" formulas, such as the National Front in the France of the 1990s and still today. To reformulate dominant pronouncements, intellectuals need at once to "free the power of their imagination while avoiding the construction of theoretical utopias" (1998: 12).

The spatial drift of these words is clear: globalization has done away with earlier dreams of universal harmony that were born of the Revolution, felt in the Marxian concept of the *cité des fins* and envisaged in the Third Republic. It was a dream, writes Balibar, to think that the unification of the human species in one single space of exchange, intellectual communication and division of labor would coincide with the resolution of racial and national antagonisms, of inequality and oppression (1998: 14). The end of the Cold War and the interpenetration of

1   All translations from *Droit de cité* are my own.

North and South have done away with such ideals. The global unity of mankind sharing the same economic problems, living under the observation of the same satellites, resembles more the Hobbesian dictum of a war of each against all, of a state of *nature* rather than a *civil space*.

For Balibar, intellectuals must shoulder the responsibility of transforming existing institutional spaces from within their national borders. Critical of the "anarchic hopes" for the withering away of the state that he finds in Deleuze and Guattari, he argues for the necessity of institutions to manage the spatial dilemmas wrought by demographic saturation and loss of sustainable resources. The Marxian strain of Balibar's inquiry bears directly at once on the material world, on experience and on individual and collective action. His work includes a psychoanalytic element when he alludes to these "fictional places" whence current burning questions are in need of being rearticulated. Furthermore, "fiction," he writes, "is the production of the real from experience [...] where insurrection opens on to the constitution (and the transformation of existing constitutions)" (1998: 15). Reformulation consists simultaneously of a critique of a collective condition *and* a performative enunciation taken as a form of action. These fictional places are constantly changing. In France in the 1990s they dealt with the nation-state in relation to the status of legal and illegal foreigners. Their situations put into conflict visible and invisible borders through the representations that French nationals and non-nationals project upon each other. Balibar resists the abolition or homogenization of differences that remain constitutive of what he continues to call, with emphasis on the plural, civilizations. The self-enclosed nation-state that insulates itself from foreign intrusions should be turned into a national and social state where borders are porous and citizenship or the practice of civic rights is not limited to nationals. Modest gains achieved in France in these areas are offset by what Balibar denounces as the *nihilism* created by globalization and exacerbated by "the media hyperspace."

Balibar sets out to find positive transformations. The French nation-state can no longer define itself as a homogeneous space against an outside, in the way it is said to have done over the last hundred years. Already in the nineteenth century, he reminds his readers, the nation-state produced not only external but also internal exclusions in the tiered structure of classes. Today, with residues of colonialism and especially the impact of economic globalization, the influx of legal and illegal migrants to France leads to new exclusions. In the 1990s, French intellectuals and citizens helped illegal immigrants, positing that citizenship is not a status but a practice. Many illegal immigrants acquired sufficient existential territory to become agents. They showed the state that it is not necessary to be a "French national" to practice good citizenship. Resistance on the part of foreigners, coupled with that of French citizens, helped to revitalize democratic politics. Their militancy has led to political activity within a new nation-state whose transnational dimension begins to open on to a global arena. As an opening perspective Balibar envisages the democratization of borders. With globalization, France, like other states now composed of many cultures, has become a country of transnational character. At the same time, a new *apartheid* is created inside its territory wherever people, kept from gainful employment, are spatially sequestered into not-so-remote areas (*banlieues*) where they live in anomie. Much in the line of Certeau and Begag, Balibar argues that internal and external borders have to be transformed.

Borders are an especially sensitive issue when the relation between France and some of its ex-colonies is considered. Algeria is a keynote: Balibar accuses those who deplore the present non-separation of the two countries of being colonialists. What if, he asks, "the spatio-temporal, or socio-temporal idea of an *irreversible* duality were the mark not of decolonization but of a persisting form of colonization?" (1998: 73). Today, France and Algeria are comprised of many diverse cultures, and they are inextricably linked through geography and history. The relation should not be thought as one of antagonism or even symmetry but, again, as one of porous reciprocity. Balibar paraphrases his friend Jacques Rancière: "To speak of the relation between France and Algeria is to speak first about France's relation to its own alterity as well as to its necessary 'disidentification' from some mythic and timeless 'Frenchness'" (Balibar 1978:74). Balibar links the state of Franco-Algerian relations to a *new* transnationalism. Classical (communist) internationalism, tied to class consciousness, failed in its attempt to construct a universal language. Today's internationalism has to begin with new ways of thinking historical correlations among nations as well as the relation between history and the very *form* of the "nation." Rather than claiming that the state does not exist, we now need to distinguish the *state* from the *nation*. To do so, we rethink the history of the constitution of Western nation-states under the banner of imperialism. The idea of empire continues to inhabit the notion of nation, even after their juridical and physical separation (1998: 80).[2] Even new nations, including Algeria, show signs of imperialism. It is crucial to begin

2 Balibar's view differs from that developed by Michael Hardt and Antonio Negri (2000). Hardt and Negri argue for a concept of "empire" that is linked to globalization and differs from the earlier colonial imperialism that depended on center and periphery.

to countenance the nation as an entity separate from its imperial heritage.

One way, Balibar says, resides less with a distance between empire and republic than with the concept of a border that never simply separates two spatial entities. Between France and Algeria there exists a *world-border* extended under the sign of a double constraint marked by the impossibility of separating *and* the necessity of being separated from each other. Foreign bodies cannot be eliminated from either side since they are all at once part of a physical presence, of memory and of a formation of identities (1998: 82). Geographical and historical constraints create a space where, as Balibar would have it, difference differs from itself and operates in key institutions. Such a difference makes possible the reinvention of politics and democracy through the representation of society within the state when it is decoupled from the nation. It affects the very process of nationalization of society by the state. We may take the example of language. Against earlier predictions, French remains an official vehicle in Algeria.[3] It necessarily includes a reference to a kind of ideal and mythic *francité*, but also, Balibar argued a decade ago, to republicanism or the untranslatable *laicité* that—unlike in former British colonies—is operative in France's ex-colonies. Conversely, within France, the growing and unstoppable influence of Arabic on popular culture is accompanied by a reflection of the century-old importance of Arabic language and culture on French intellectual life.[4]

Of even greater importance, complicated family structures and genealogies erase an easy distinction between public and private space at the same time as they defy official administrative practices (1998: 82). Privately, many Franco-Algerian families bear a double identity with political consequences that often lead to violence. As the result of the transportation of the *harkis*—the Algerians who fought on the side of the French—and the integration of immigrant labor following the Algerian war of independence, both countries and all classes of society share *and* divide (*partagent*) more and more families.[5] The constraint creates problems for a concept of the state as an enveloping unity in which genealogies are both instituted and protected (1998: 83). Private structures are

---

3 This is the view Albert Memmi puts forward in *The Colonizer and the Colonized* (1957). Memmi revises some of his earlier findings in his *Decolonization and the Decolonized* (2004).

4 See, for example, "Al Djazaïr, une année de l'Algérie en France," January–December, 2003, a year of symbolic cultural events to show the relations between two countries both linked and opposed by history.

5 *Harkis* is the name given to the Algerians who fought on the side of the French. After independence, they were given the opportunity of going to France to avoid death. The history of the *harkis* is only beginning to be discussed.

embedded in the public institutions they transform.

The increased development of transnational links, that is, of links beyond the borders of a national space, is the effect both of postcolonialism and, now, of globalization. These links often reveal economic inequalities that introduce relations of power in a world that relativizes national sovereignties in the North and South. How will such a political and economic context affect "cultural" confrontations? This question bears on the place of Islam, to begin with, in the Franco-Algerian structure. While noting the exclusion of Islam from French public space, Balibar sees the politicization of religion as a response to global processes of modernization.

His provocative conclusions establish Balibar's position as a French, a European and a global intellectual. How, he asks in 1997, can transnational, collective identities search for alternatives to what he insists on calling "Americanization" in a global context? "Americanization," we recall from Baudrillard, is synonymous with the imposition of a homogeneous economic and political model. Islam, Balibar argues, is not simply the substitution of a traditional nationalism but, rather, a way of asking for *another* universality to be placed next to the dominant, exclusive, American model (1998: 85). Islam can be seen as denouncing the very element of particularism that might be affiliated with individuals and their existential territories. If some of these remarks have to be modified after 9/11, Balibar's conclusion that the ideological world-scene is not that of a conflict between a universalism and particularisms but, on the contrary, the scene of conflicts between *fictive* universalities and struggles within Western universalism itself continues to hold.

Citizen-Subjects

All these questions have spatial implications that are linked to mental and physical territories, to nation-states and, as Balibar continually notes, to borders. Whereas nation-states are comprised of ever-more transnational links, borders become increasingly problematic when they are viewed from various angles at once. How is it possible to transform the notion of a border in relation to political spaces aside from making them more porous? Since, Balibar argues, citizenship will not be entirely separated from nationality in the foreseeable future, and borders will not vanish overnight, how today does the state condition both subjectivity and citizenship? Can citizenship go beyond nationality so as to relativize it in the best of global ways?

Identity is necessary but it is bestowed not only by nationality: other, private layers, including the family, the employer, the political party, sports and professional associations, offer many possibilities for the invention of existential territories. Identities today are increasingly multiple, though, for Balibar, they are *not* as "romantically free-flowing" as many post-structuralist thinkers would have had it; nor are humans simply "formatted," as Latour would say, with the "double-click" of a mouse. The identities Balibar outlines differ from "identitarian identities," be they nationalistic, ethnic, religious or related to special interest groups (1998: 21). In the case of identitarian identities, terms such as "French," "patriot," "Muslim" or "foreigner" function as signs that have been emptied of their content. Identities must be linked to active, spatial practices in and against which they function transversally, between layers (e.g., Latour's networks).

With the rapid transformation of the nation-state, what new institutions of citizenship, asks Balibar, will advance both the right to difference *and* to differ from difference? Current identity conflicts in France and elsewhere are too often short-circuited into identitarian conflicts that raise questions of security and violence with, as he puts it sarcastically, "a little zest of humanitarianism" (1998: 129–30). Humans have the right to difference, equality, solidarity and community. It is not a question of making identities disappear but of giving individuals and groups the means and the opportunities to identify and "*dis*-identify," that is, to open mental and physical *spaces* and to *travel* in their identities.

In France, Balibar asserts in 1998, such a new institution of citizenship will come about if the Franco-Algerian pairing becomes one of the privileged elements in the country's political meditations. This unit cannot be achieved in a dual, purely antagonistic relation or outside of the context of globalization. Writing at a time when the border separating the two countries had become a site of extreme violence, he decries the fact that while goods and ideas circulate, and while many Algerians have a vital need to cross national borders, some French citizens retain a Maginot mentality to ensure their security. He argues strongly for a *political* practice of borders that would no longer be off-limits to popular contestations vital for democracy. Borders are never controlled collectively but always by those in power. They are made in order to control certain citizens and populations and to encourage passage by others. How can this be turned around? How can borders become a political site in such a way that citizens can negotiate their practice and bring about transformation? Who, we might ask, are the citizens in this case? Do they include immigrants and non-nationals? Do the latter have a voice in deciding on visible and invisible borders and their control? Balibar skirts the issue. He argues for a new civilizing project that would help reconstruct, beyond simple national and world borders, the entire Mediterranean region, where, at the end of the twentieth century, there remains violent conflict among cultures within the world-space (1998: 88). Balibar argues for the necessity of a new civility that for him is linked to a *droit de cité*, a crucial term in his idiolect, which means the right to dwell and to move as a subject and a citizen.[6] The shared etymology of civility, *cité* and citizen is enough to urge French citizens to civilize *themselves* rather than to export civilization to others as in the days of colonialism.

Such a civilizing project, based on a reinvention of culture and politics and the transformation of the nation-state and borders, constitutes a multilayered spatial practice. The reinvention of politics takes place at several distinct levels that cannot be conflated. The first level is that of citizenship. The goal of citizenship is to obtain adequate representation of individuals, groups and legitimate interests in society and institutions in order to rebuild a state that, without having disappeared, has lost much of its power to transnational investments. In a long and provocative article entitled "Citizen-Subject" (1991), Balibar traces the history of the citizen and the subject in Western thinking. Critical of Heidegger and others whose hypotheses he reverses, he argues that the citizen is always a supposed subject (legal, psychological, transcendental) (1991: 45). Nuancing Jean-Luc Nancy's historical distinction between the monarchic subject and the republican citizen, he introduces the working hypothesis that the subject depends on the revolutionary citizen in order to be: "The citizen can be simultaneously considered as the constitutive element of the State and as the actor of a revolution" (1991: 54). Acknowledging his debt to Michel Foucault's utopian thinking, Balibar concludes that

> to understand that this subject (which the citizen will be supposed to be) contains the paradoxical unity of a universal sovereignty and a radical finitude, we must envisage his constitution—in all the historical complexity of the practices and symbolic forms which it brings together—from both the point of view of the State apparatus and that of the permanent revolution. This ambivalence is his strength, his historical ascendancy. (1991: 55)

Today we can wonder about this historical figure of the citizen-subject

6 The Italian philosopher Gianni Vattimo coined the expression *Il pensiero debole*, soft thinking (1988), which was taken up by several French intellectuals such as Guattari and Balibar. To combat and prevent violence, one has to act softly or, as here, with civility.

and whether it will be replaced by another. It is important more than ever to retain a subject with a symbolic or existential dimension so that citizens will not become mere samples or pawns in a market economy. Their means to control the latter's powers, Balibar argues, have decreased dramatically since 1989. Rather than declaring that the nation-state is a thing of the past, citizens must ask themselves how it has been changed and how in turn they can change it. The situation has become more difficult at a time when institutions and places of decision on which citizens depend are situated simultaneously at local, national and transnational levels. Citizens have to strive for effective representation and for control of power at all levels (1998: 126).

All citizens are currently required to struggle for representation but none more so than foreigners. What will the representation of foreigners be in national politics? In France, as economic globalization progresses and other traditional sectors of citizenship consolidate, the space given to foreigners diminishes. The right of foreigners to speak in a public space is disappearing. Foreigners must become not only people *for* whom, but *with* whom French nationals speak and act. The French cannot look, as if from the outside, at movements such as those of the young *beur* or of the Africans from the *banlieue*. Such a posture contributes to the renewed status of foreigners as "strangers" to be excluded from the nation. It erects invisible borders inside a territory and institutes a spatial apartheid for those who are, in fact, not only citizens but in many cases also nationals (1998: 127). Since the urban turmoil of 2005 and 2007, Balibar's words now seem prophetic. Youth in the *banlieue* live in an anomie invisible to those residing in the city. They live outside of what Virilio called "the new social pyramid." Their rage—or *haine*—is often directed against their own surroundings.[7]

Civility and European Citizenship

The problems facing the French nation-state are similar to those experienced by other members of the European Union. Balibar sees the regulation of migrants from outside of the EU—and, at times, even from within—as constituting a new form of colonialism (Balibar et al. 1999).

---

7   Mathieu Kassovitz's film *La haine* (Hate) (1995) shows that hate and violence in the *banlieue* was what first shook up the sleepy French bourgeois. The riots of October 2005 were triggered—after a summer of tensions between police and youth—by the deaths of two teenagers. They began in Clichy-sous-Bois near Paris and soon spread to all poor suburbs in France.

The continued equation of citizenship with nationality has increasingly discriminatory consequences. Borders reinforce a selection between rich and poor. A growing national as well as a worldwide apartheid replaces and intensifies that of the halcyon days of colonialism. Democracy, he writes just before 9/11, can only exist when borders *between* nations and *inside* each nation are liberalized. In order to guarantee social rights with a transnational character, citizenship must be separated from nationality, addressed from above *and* from below, both by the state and by a popular interest if collective agency is to be reintroduced (Balibar 2001: 180–81). Democratization of borders calls for their permeation. Structures of domination have to be abolished and spatial conditions created for political action (2001: 183–84). Such a milieu is not possible without either civility or political action that extends citizenship and the *institutional* recognition of equal rights.

The realization of Balibar's spatial model would help to reorient globalization away from the production of immensely violent forms of insecurity, away from its aversion to collective emancipation and, finally, away from new and existing structures of domination. The infrastructure of this argument is found in Hannah Arendt's notion of the "*Sans-Etats,*" or stateless people, and in Marie-Claire Caloz-Tschopp's notion of "the right to rights." To these we can also add Jacques Rancière's "*la part des sans part,*" that is, the portion of the portionless (1995). Arendt saw exclusion from citizenship as equal to the loss of human rights. Citizenship guarantees the very basis for human rights, when all is said and done, which concern a simple right to existence (Balibar 2001: 187). Today the loss or non-existence of these rights puts *subhumans* next to *superhumans*. Balibar sees this new division as an irreversible and growing phenomenon in Europe and the world. He continues to valorize a politics that for him is not a superstructure imposed on social structures. It is the very condition of exchange insofar as it institutes a *space of encounter*, of formulation and resolution of antagonisms, that is, of the very "*being in common*" of the different components of humanity (2001: 188–89). An ongoing *re*-creation of civility across all visible and invisible borders is necessary to produce areas of encounter and to inaugurate new common spaces.

It is incumbent upon the European Union to modify its current politics of a selective acceptance of humans that reduces migrants and asylum seekers to second-class citizens (2001: 191). Given the climate of global violence and a "politics of non-intervention" adopted toward a series of brutal conflicts since the 1990s (such as Rwanda, to which, now, many more examples may be added, from Sudan to Zimbabwe), as well as new restrictions on immigration everywhere, Balibar wonders, prior to the war in Iraq, if such a politics of civility could even exist in today's world, where those who reside inside the new social pyramid refuse to recognize those who are outside, who are often immigrants or descendants of immigrants. Asking what kind of citizenship would be possible in the new national and transnational spaces of Europe, Balibar distinguishes between two models that are currently available. In the first, humans exist only through social relations that both link and oppose them to one another. From one social state to another, individuals have more or less freedom to move between a set of appurtenances. Inspired by Arendt and even distantly by Martin Heidegger, Balibar's second model pushes to the limit the notion of a *communauté de destin*, a "community of fate." This model considers that humans and the historical and cultural groups they constitute are thrown as if "naked" into a public space. They actively and continually have to reconstruct this mental and physical space of encounter in order to disinter the very conditions of existence that make possible the construction of common and communal spaces. The second model lays more stress on the active participation of the citizen by underlining the fact that citizenship is not a status but a sum of practices that define each citizen's relation to herself or himself and to others through solidarity and reciprocity. The "community of fate" emphasizes contingency and the conflictual conditions of politics. Instead of the invisible violence of consensus, true democracy needs conflict that can be collectively managed.[8] Community, synonymous with a space of exchange, can only be practiced in cognizance of the contradictions of individual and collective subjectivities. In order to have true reciprocity, the so-called natives *and* the new arrivals have to *reconstruct* their community at every moment through the political imagination as it applies to new domains or situations, new territories or city-spaces (2001: 214). The idea of imperfection is both positive and productive, since what is perfect would have no need for imagination or the invention of new ecological spaces.[9]

However, under the sign of reciprocity this hypothetically active space of encounter is threatened by a renewed racism, the result of migration caused by uneven economic development. Similar situations exist today

8 On the violence of consensus, see also Jacques Rancière in *Aesthetics and Its Discontents* (2004).

9 In his late work, especially *Rogues: Two Essays on Reason* (2003), Jacques Derrida puts democracy in a millenarian frame when, by way of Maurice Blanchot, he writes of a *démocratie à venir*, a democracy to come that is experienced as a promise that is distinct from concrete democracy. Derrida also argues that democracy, no matter how imperfect, is nonetheless the only system of governance that has room for change and improvement.

in many countries not only in Europe but all over the world, from Dubai to China, from Qatar to Botswana and Singapore to the United States. In Europe this state of things is currently linked to collective rights, the difference between nationality and citizenship and the treatment of what are still called "minorities." The political frame belonging to all of Europe (Balibar 2002: 242) enters into a conflict with another that arises from global competition, in which outsourcing and flexible capital development cause the erosion of the rights that the citizens of European nations had acquired. Almost a decade later, with economic turmoil in several European countries, Balibar is more pessimistic about Europe as a "project." He insists, however, that the only possibility for Europe will be a new foundation that would give the continent some geopolitical leverage. As he recently writes, this can come about on one condition only, that is, if

> all the challenges involved in the idea of an original form of post-national federation are seriously and courageously met. These involve setting up a common public authority, which is neither a state nor a simple "governance" of politicians and experts; securing genuine equality among the nations, thus fighting against reactionary nationalisms; and above all reviving democracy in the European space, thus resisting the current process of "de-democrati-zation" or "statism without a State" produced by neo-liberalism. (2000: 242, my translation)

For Balibar, an invasive market economy and global liberalism threaten the very principles of democracy.

Global Spaces

In 1989 the Western media exploited the destruction of the Berlin Wall to peddle the illusion of a world unified under the banner of economic and cultural liberalism. However, since the events of 9/11 the world is less clearly unified than had been suggested twelve years earlier, and the consequence is that national borders are less permeable than before. Balibar sees the need for intellectuals to tender to the world at large the idea of a new universality that would differ from the earlier particularist universalities, which amounted to pockets of regional ideology. He hopes that this new universality—not to be confused with a media-generated cosmopolitanism or the Marxist myth of unification—will result from a productive encounter and debate. It will consist of many conflicting universalities that can co-exist only through ongoing negotiation and translation. Intellectuals have to lend a critical ear to objections and demands that reach them from other parts of their city, their country, the

European continent but also the world, be it east, south or west, to denounce repressive social, cultural and political spaces as well as to create new ones (2003: 5).

To achieve this, power relations have to be examined to see how they can be modified in view of global *decentralization*. Given the urgency of the situation and the speed with which the world moves, intellectuals have to translate their thoughts directly into action. Thought-action involves the ongoing recreation of social, cultural and political spaces where, because of its history, Europe—rather than simply the "West"— is well positioned to bring about a redistribution of global power. Other modifications will refine the ongoing invention of citizenship as a *process* and not as a finality. Conflicts in social space, often resulting from migration, have to be seen as internal, rather than external, to the French and other European states. New rights and positive liberties have to be granted to citizens so as to increase their *capacities* (2003: 40). Political lessons are easily threatened when France and other European states turn to transnational corporatism at the very moment when deregulation and globalization of the economy deprive them of the means to protect their own citizens against the fluctuations of the market.

These dilemmas (but they are productive ones) are part of a dynamic process that is renewing the European cultural and political experience. Its character requires Europe to engage in a project of transformation of international relations. This transformation is built upon an economic base, to be sure, but also on cultural, intellectual, social and institutional forces that are both interior and exterior to the European space. Balibar envisions a new Europe tending to commit to a regime of power in which no one has the exclusive proprietary right over others. Such a power would translate itself more gently through the evolution of certain structures and relations of power from the *inside* so as to produce alternatives to a dominant course based solely on economics. Balibar hopes that this "anti-strategy" will transform international relations slowly and—albeit with reversals—unmistakably. Change must begin from a mutual trust between heterogeneous populations and improved communication—this includes negotiations as well as translation between heterogeneous populations. They have to be both global and regional. Unlike the city centers favored by economic globalism, the regional components would depend on their own genesis and be held together culturally and historically. The global counterpart could be thought of as the matrix for the beginning of *another* form of globalization—distinct from the more folkloristic *alter-mondialisation*—that would exploit technology to develop new forms of civility.

Territories and Common Spaces

How, Balibar asks, is it possible to construct new social, cultural and political territories that are at once private and public, mental and physical? A citizen's rights are needed for the creation of an existential territory from which to speak and act. In France, the European Union and elsewhere the major obstacle continues to be posed by legal and illegal migrants and, increasingly, by threats of terrorism. The problems are both local and global, the result of social and economic inequities. In France, the United Kingdom and, to a lesser degree, Germany, migrants are also inscribed in a postcolonial history. Their claims are written in legal rights and in a cultural space. Migrants in France do not just ask for "mobility" but also for a right to dwell (*droit de cité*) that includes the right to circulate and to speak in public forums. They are not a flowing, floating mass but travelers who, having been forced to move, are at times liberated but more often are targets of discrimination. Their demands are continually rejected, but in no way are they annihilated.

However, migration always presupposes an evolution of the relation between subject and territory that the democratization of inner and outer borders can alter in the best of ways. Balibar argues *for* circulation and mixing, processes that, for him, civilize and democratize. Europe is given the chance to carry out decolonization on its own territory by struggling against various forms of *provincialism*, not to be associated with regionalism, by participating in the construction of a new universalism on a basis that would be more "republican." A few examples are proposed. A new universality would be a founding idea of international solidarity from below, from an increasingly transnational, civil society, *and* from above, from the state or an alliance of several states. Whether France, Europe or a global world-space, citizens, intellectuals and responsible governments would engage in common thought and action. Grassroot movements *and* those in decision-making positions have to work together in solidarity to construct common spaces.

Balibar again makes a case not only for disarmament but for establishing norms for the protection of the environment and, related to this, for a regulation of economic planning that would replace the principle of unlimited accumulation of wealth with that of sustainable development. This new universality would also extend to the struggle against collective discrimination founded on anthropological differences ("race" or ethnicity, gender or sex, but also age and state of health) or the status of cultural, national and religious majorities as well as minorities, as is inscribed in the fundamental mission of the United Nations. Though this is required from all states according to their constitutions, its application in practice has been turned upside down by decolonization, international migration and the globalization of communication.[10]

Intellectuals in the Picture of Culture

Two questions arise concerning the definition of intellectuals as subjects and citizens and, as is the case with every intellectual, the role that art plays in the international matrix. Intellectuals are not simply deterritorialized souls. They are inscribed in geographical, geopolitical and historical contexts and by definition are travelers. They write from their own national contexts, replete with geographical and historical implications, at the same time as they open on to and intersect with others in the wider context of France in Europe and in its ex-colonies. Intellectuals bear the responsibility of thinking and acting directly from events. With a nod to a Deleuzian idiolect, Balibar adds that intellectuals think only through difference and rectification. Migrating among family structures, professional and political organizations, between cultures and countries, they actively practice "dis-identification" from standard, clichéd— "dominant"—models of thinking. Balibar countenances intellectuals as travelers rather than as *nomads* who, in his mind, are too removed from *concrete* social and political situations. He finds that Deleuze's concept of "nomadism," like that of smooth space on which it finds ground, can all too readily be joined to "capitalist hyperspace."

Balibar imagines intellectuals to be "vanishing mediators" (an expression borrowed from Fredric Jameson) who mediate and build only in order to themselves disappear. Translators all, intellectuals also move through and along the interstices of languages and cultures. Cultural translation entails the search for equivalences and ethical, aesthetic, technological and epistemological universals that lead ultimately to the

---

10 Balibar offers concrete definitions of a secular universality. He strongly opposes the current reactivation of theological conflicts and the reduction of collective identities to models of religious belonging and territories that would compete with national spaces and social classes. He remains optimistic. Even if religious groups challenge UNESCO or WHO, it seems to him unlikely that religion will take over international institutions. Faced with the religious fervor of terrorism and global counter-terrorism which both sanctify armed conflict and equate the enemy with the devil, a concerted effort has to be made to secularize politics. Balibar mobilized Jacques Derrida to argue for the necessity of a critique of religion based on the invention of a new Enlightenment, neither as an expression of an occidental particularism nor as the secularization of theological concepts (2003: 189).

recognition of cultural incompatibilities. Gone are the days when as self-styled leaders intellectuals believed they could speak in place of or for the masses. Now the intellectual-translator subverts an earlier critical function that had conferred upon the intellectual the mantle of a judge, a priest, a member of a vigilante committee or a censor. To the current, derivative, indeed trivialized and commercialized usage of "culture" (which Certeau had analyzed with caustic clarity, 1997b: 101–05) Balibar prefers "art," which he understands as a Brechtian effect of distancing intended to reveal conflicts of identity occurring both in the spectator *and* on their outside. Art distances its participants in order to have them regulate their own conflicts, including those, in psychoanalytic terms, of "another scene" in which the unconscious is shown regulating cultures and societies. Distancing is a spatial category that dramatizes conflicts of identity that are invariably grounded in fictional places (*lieux de fiction*).

Next to Brecht's theater, Balibar subscribes to a cinema that politicizes its topics in deep space: Roberto Rossellini and the Italian neo-realists; the French New Wave in the line of Godard; Mizoguchi and much of Japanese cinema. Today such distancing is scarcely to be found either on television or in commercial film simply because the media disallow any performance that would enable humans to gain perspective on the very construction of identity, first, in the global context and, secondly, in its relation to the various places where humans live (1998: 132). Art includes stories that, Balibar argues, spatialize and temporalize each work from the inside. A story may include simultaneously the people it represents, the artist and the spectator as well. Humans cannot dominate the image or the text with a discourse that would be exterior to the world or to the work of art, such as a theory or a history of culture.

Through what Balibar writes of art and aesthetics, it is clear that the *becoming* of a world-space is unpredictable: "The global collapse of metalanguage, including that of revolutionary metalanguage that dreamed of enclosing the future of humanity and its representations in the order-words of a single collective subject—a fortiori that of the communicational metalanguage—is not the end of historicity" (1998: 160). The more that images proliferate, the more they speak. The multiple possibilities of their composition (*possibilités d'assemblage*) refer to historical constructions and cultural practices. No longer a given, history is unpredictable and can be constructed anywhere. Art thus tells us that globalization is not to be equated with the imposition of a single discourse. On the contrary, it replaces totalization with the proliferation of many discourses. How does this state of things affect what is seen as the decomposition of identities and of a traditional universalism? Rather than either embracing or lamenting the fact of deterritorialization, Balibar finds it productive to show that both extremes belong to a process of overdetermination, what he calls, in the words of Deleuze and Guattari, *transversal* analyses that take into consideration impersonal economic processes *and* processes of subjectivation. The newly globalized world (the old one began with the discovery of the Americas) is neither one of transparency and translatability of a universal language advertised by the communications and media companies, nor is it one of incommunicability or untranslatability, be it of social classes or of ethnic, religious and aesthetic cultures. A remainder is what spurs the very desire to continue communicate. Cultures are singular but they can be communicated and translated.[11]

In sum, Balibar envisions the construction of a new space (*nouvel espace*) in the age of economic globalization in which the state is no longer a leading player. The subject who invents his or her ecological spaces no longer militates against the state but actively and as a citizen undoes the visible and invisible borders that surround the state and criss-cross its surface arenas. Balibar argues for the genesis of a space, be it a state or a region, in a networked world where all changes must come from within through ongoing travel, translation and negotiation. Reaffirming the importance of intellectuals, Balibar notes that in a world of acceleration, the latter have to translate thought directly into action and continually adapt their critical thinking. They address increasingly transnational issues where private and public spaces are more and more intertwined. Their responsibility is to undo social injustices in a de-centered world where a former universalism has been replaced with myriad, often competing, universalities. To this end, they need to travel mentally and physically as well as to translate cultural and social differences. They are mediators and negotiators who institute a climate of civility in an increasingly militarized world-space. Emphasizing geopolitics and a quasi-existential way of being in the world, he exhorts his public to resist this tendency and to create ecological territories based on a new universalism. Though he recognizes the force of networks of the kind that Bruno Latour has studied, he chooses not to address changes that accelerating communications may bring to subjectivity. Whatever their form may be, subjectivities must be seen in the context of increasing cultural and social

---

11 Like Certeau (Chapter 2), Balibar argues that some codes translate easily while others pertaining to symbolic matters—life, death, sexuality, gender, even law—do not (1995: 774–99).

métissage or hybridization. Because alterity is anthropological and political, the dyad of self and other now translates into citizens and noncitizens. If new spaces are invented they will figure in the sphere of geopolitics. If they are also existential and ecological, as they would be for the classical thinkers who inaugurated this study, they may belong to times past and thus become what, "out of the past," is crucial for invention in our shrinking world. Their fiction, like Balibar's it is hoped, will become our reality.

Conclusion: Future Spaces

Nothing looks the same. Space is different and so is time. Space is now that of a fully urbanized planet Earth.

Bruno Latour

It is strange to read Bruno Latour, an aficionado of the great wines that his family cultivates in the rolling hills of southern Burgundy, noting that the world is now entirely urbanized. A constructively paranoid response to his assertion, similar to statements by Edward Soja, an urbanist who argues for planetary urbanization, is that little is left for ecology. Latour appeals to hyperbole to argue that the planet will be entirely urbanized. The virtue of this overstatement is found in the fact that the distinction between the country and the city no longer holds, and as a result its argument can be a prompt for a continued *variegation* of space, which might constitute the basis for an informed sense of ecology that results from close study of the spatial crises that come with globalization. Latour notes that our world is understood less through the information we can gather about it than through the ongoing transformations we witness happening to it. Our perception of the distribution of sites, states and world-space exists only through recognition of rapid and ever-changing alignments, distributions, modes of formatting, and of linking and narrating.

The chapters above have sought to gain a sense of the alignments and their shifts. The method has entailed assembling, reassembling, comparing and contrasting nine French theorists—a mix of philosophers, anthropologists, sociologists, historians and public intellectuals—whose reflections on space bear on ecology in the sense of habitability. All of them lead us to a threshold where our own spatial condition can be reconsidered. What dynamisms can we take from their theories to assist us today in thinking what future spaces are possible? And what, we are tempted to ask, is the future of space in general? In the post-war period and especially after 1968, the theorists examined here felt that the world into which they were born was far from the one they had come to know and that, they felt, they would later experience in the course of their lives. The shift from the post-war era to that of globalization—what one geographer has defined as "the sum of processes whose activity is neither ruled nor interpreted according to the categories of space and time that during

145

the modern era conditioned the understanding of what takes place"
(Farinelli 2009: 50)—led them, each in respect to his own discipline and
methodology, urgently to re-evaluate its conceptual ground. All appear
to share common preoccupations. They focus first on a perceived loss of
anthropological—by which is meant symbolic and existential—space,
first under the rule of a monolithic state and now, increasingly, as a result
of what seems to be an orchestrated governmental stalemate in collusion
with a new order or corporate law. They count among those who first
perceived the effects of globalization that we are witnessing today.

Two burning ecological questions in the second half of the twentieth
century have been, first, how to reinvent and practice space in such a way
as to escape the grip that the administrative state (as "State") holds on
its subjects; and, secondly, how to obviate the effects of imposed
consumerism and media-driven propaganda in the service of the transnational corporate economy. To counter the homogenizing effects of
governmental administration, several of these critics advocated the
creation of spatial practices through the simple and time-held tactics of
dialogue, in the narration of their experience in the post-war culture, and
their embrace of counter-movements or of various biopolitics that shape
everyday life. Thus, outside (or falling beneath the radar) of state order
and reason these writers imagine and develop existential territories in
otherwise degrading situations. Close inspection revealed that another
symbolic order, rife with discrimination, generally subjugating women
and minorities, cuts through what we have called "anthropological"
spaces. The governing apparatus of the state was exactly what post-1968
theorists first felt to be the cause of social inequity. The same critics soon
realized that, just as the state weakens under the impact of global
economic transformations, so also do its subjects find themselves
deprived of the spaces their oppositional or inventive art had crafted.
They see themselves packaged as market samples or reduced to raw data.
In reaction, and from a variety of angles, they envisage the creation of
space in view of an ecological ethics.

The Western city that since the Renaissance had served as the background of countless novels and poems has been seen as slowly collapsing.
Extending into an amorphous urban sprawl, its perimeters have disappeared. The effect, as Lefebvre had presciently shown, is to erase the
division between country and city that had been part of the Western
compass for almost a millennium. So important to the society under state
regulation, which Lefebvre saw everywhere imprinting its symbolic and
patriarchal emblem, subjects (maintained Michel de Certeau) tend to lose
both the existential territories they created and the concurrent—and

vital—illusion of life as marked by a perceived substance or depth. Long-held hierarchies that persisted after the Second World War, Jean Baudrillard observes, unravel in a functionalist world where subjects are carried off in a general circulation of signs. Based on the influx of new and often toxic money, unforeseen hierarchies are imposed. In this kind of "postmodern" atmosphere, other critics analyze the illusory space that electronic media and advertisements circulate on a transnational scale. According to Marc Augé, in the age of the "supermodern" in which we are living a human being has to learn to reconsider space as he or she never had before. Other theorists deplore the increased manipulation that the media exercise upon subjects and denounce the resulting loss of the rights they had as citizens. Analyzing at the same time the compression of space and time under the impact of speed which reduced human spatial scales to an urban instant, the pollution of both the mind and the planet as an effect of consumerism, Paul Virilio notes that what is needed is the reinvention of "political man."

Drawing on these often wry, polemical and dire assessments of the human condition, other critics (Gilles Deleuze and Félix Guattari, Bruno Latour and Etienne Balibar) continue to analyze and look for ways to cut through or out of the oppressive conditions in which, they claim variously, humans are entrenched. In the wake of Virilio, they are aware that theory has to insert itself into today's conditions. In view of galloping urbanization, billowing transnational markets and the accelerated creations of electronic technology, Deleuze and Guattari called for a generalized thinking in which "rhizomes" can change the order of inherited social conventions and networks of communication. As much a way of thinking as the virtual mapping of a counter-movement, the rhizome belongs to the lexicon describing the synthesis of mental and physical ecology. It is a diagram for perpetually bifurcating itineraries that move across and through areas of social contradiction.

Like the authors of *A Thousand Plateaus* and *The Three Ecologies*, Latour and Balibar elaborate ecological spaces by way of their utopian thinking or by what I have chosen to call their "spatial fictions." Each finds that the opening of new spaces, however difficult it may be in an era of marketing, is vital for the survival of humans and the planet. Both have condemned consensus, the bedrock of the ethic of consumerism and, no less, the yoking of flexible capital and media that enables wholesale exploitation of humans and irreversible destruction of the planet. For Latour and Balibar electronic transmission of information (which generally carries propaganda) increasingly affects the coordinates of space and time with which subjectivities are mapped. Rather than simply being dominated by them, humans will find that machines, Latour predicts, will overtake their own mental and physical capacities. The oppression that we witness in the contemporary world, he continues, is often the result of outmoded modernist concepts that the West inherits and perpetuates because it functions according to antiquated models of control while refusing the reality of feedback loops. The West—the collective noun is Latour's—continues to believe that history is linear and that concepts such as science, nature and reason, along with their avatars including technology, democracy and the market, are universal. What if, Latour declares, multiculturalism found an echo in what might be called "multinaturalism"?

What if, we can ask somewhat less romantically, the Western universalism that modernism had predicated were replaced by another concept, a concept consisting of many different universalities or what Lefebvre had called "differentials"? Since three watershed dates—1968, 1989 and especially 2001—it has become apparent that humans live in "different worlds" that are perpetually at war with one another. Any peace, if peace there can be, has to be continually negotiated. In such a climate of local conflict everywhere on the planet Latour and Balibar countenance theorists and intellectuals more and more as diplomats called upon to negotiate and translate their personal and cultural differences with others in an ongoing and open-ended way so as collaborate and invent spaces in common and to render the world habitable. The *new ecological spaces* they help construct cannot be imposed from the top down but have to be born from within and through negotiation. They would undo anthropological distinctions, legacies of the modernist era that produced exclusions based primarily on gender and race but also on age and health.

Yet no one can entirely espouse, as Latour would have it, an electronic mobility and a simple formatting of the kind that relinquishes the differentiation between a self, a subject, and its other: for today it is a social fact that human communities cannot function at all without the permeable and even impermeable barriers that define their members and the alterities they share from within and without. The experience of Facebook, LinkedIn and other technologies of encounter shows that subjects who live within the matrices of electronic technologies multiply their identities; they become less stable than in "cold" societies where they remained more firmly embedded in kinship structures. Now, however, they can indeed be said to move along networks and may even appear to live in Virilio's "urban instant." If, to undo the mental and physical compression that a consumerist media politics imposes, they seek to "practice" space in the modes that Lefebvre and Certeau had theorized, it will be less in the street than in the new media streams. Yet they still do not completely give up a kernel of self and its unconscious, even with the loss of delay, deferment (or feedback). Moreover, in order to gain access, as Lefebvre and Certeau would have it, to an *art* of everyday life (in which the unconscious can play a role), subjects have to gain the sense of a minimal existential territory in and from which to live. The latter emerges only when it carries the guarantee of an incontrovertible *right*. The citizen-subject, a figure that has to be seen in ongoing transformation, is vital, as Balibar asserts, in an era when, because of transnational economic policies imposed upon masses all over the globe, many lose any possibility of access to rights that they have never acquired. In France in particular, and in the West more generally, cultural discourses have long ago been separated from political discourses, much in the way that those of the sciences took leave of the humanities in the course of the seventeenth and eighteenth centuries. The reinvention of "citizen-subjects" from the remains of a "political man" cannot be achieved without thinking through issues such as *habitus* and habitability, in other words, without opening a space from which to do so. Thus the renewed emphasis on the concept of space in the 1960s is more than simply a "spatial turn." With the perceived acceleration and shrinking of the world since 1968 whence we began, spatial and temporal coordinates have entirely changed, even if the transformation seems at first to have bypassed many cultures. The challenge facing theorists is how to reorient their thinking and their practices in relation to these new configurations.

In the treatment above I chose to focus on French writer-thinkers who have addressed the mutations of the concept of space from the 1960s to the present. Increasingly aware that they have shifted their formerly universalist claims to address local and global issues in today's world-space, they all assume that subjective and political alterities are threaded through each other. Dilemmas experienced on a personal or local scale call attention to their counterparts in other places and in other idioms. Hence the necessity of translation and negotiation as a basis for dialogue and collaboration: whether from Paris, New York, Rio, Lagos or Beijing, those who deal with virtual and actual space are enjoined to consider changes that come where electronic technologies are made available at once to a general public of "users" and to others who find themselves at different strata of economic development.

The ever-multiplying media spaces do not all have to be confused with consumerist hyperspace. Critics would be misguided if they were to refuse to recognize and even embrace *other* ways of thinking and using space, whether they be elsewhere on the globe, in what in the eyes of many had been formerly exotic places, in areas of difference within a given nation, above all in developing nations, almost invariably ex-colonies once rich with resources and populations, places at the disposal of those who claimed them as their own. These spaces need to be considered through the theory as well as the practice of a generalized sense of translation. Certeau—along with Begag—and Balibar focused primarily on movements that led from the ex-colonies to Paris and, somewhat inversely, from America to the rest of the world. Today, however, demographic flows span the globe so pervasively that the concept of hemisphere, continent or island no longer holds. If, for the critic of French extraction, migrations were often thought to occur between European nations and their ex-colonies, today they are happening in every azimuth: Peruvians migrate to Spain, Brazilians seek their fortune in Japan, Filipinos sail to Singapore, Indians migrate to the United Arab Emirates, and Africans trek to China. New—call them motley, hybrid, variegated, dappled—cultures are formed every day, and formed with them are new contours of inclusion, exclusion and racial and ethnic thinking.[1] The problems that Certeau, Balibar and others signaled regarding ethnic economies now happen multilaterally and on a global scale.

The lines of thinking about ecological spaces that these theorists follow often tend to grow out of a background of physical and historical geography that addresses dilemmas in the area of geopolitics and, by implication (although often stated *sotto voce*), ecology. Economic geographer David Harvey writes unflaggingly about "spaces of hope" in the midst of economic misery, while urbanist Edward Soja appeals to "spatial justice" to correct the inequities of uneven development—all the while prolonging a modernist perspective focusing almost exclusively on social relations. Latour reminds us that it will be of the utmost importance in an age of electronic networks to keep in mind that people continue to live in *concrete* spaces and that, if cities are to be made habitable, they need water, clean air and access to broadband for the maintenance of infrastructure and the circulation of information. Indeed, as Latour writes, since the 1960s "[n]othing looks the same. Space is different and so is time. Space is now that of a fully urbanized planet Earth" (2010: 126).

In his introduction to *Ecological Urbanism* (2010), Mohsen Mostafavi argues that where habitability lays stress on sustainability—while

---

1 In a multipolar world, Europe or even the United States is no longer the immigrant's dream-place. Tristan Coloma (2010: 12–13) has documented the attraction of China for African migrants and the severe discrimination to which they are subjected.

avoiding the corporate appropriation of the term[2]—a pressing and delicate philosophical question arises. When thinking how to make the world habitable, we have to appeal to an *ecosophy*, a word Mostafavi borrows from Félix Guattari's *Three Ecologies*. In this context, in which the condition of our *oikos* is at stake, it is fitting to invoke again the late philosopher's distinctions between mental, social and natural ecologies. What today is meant by *to domesticate* or *to make habitable*, as we have seen, is light years away from Heidegger's concept of "dwelling," a term tinged with nostalgia and, rooted as it is in the heritage of ancient Greek philosophy, unabashed Eurocentrism. Furthermore, related as it is to an ethos or *habitus*, ecology cannot simply be reduced to a technocratic question. *Contra* Heidegger, we can once more recall Guattari who replaced the former Marxist concepts of infrastructure and superstructure with regimes of signs (at once economic, juridical and scientific) bearing on subjectivation, in other words, on the ways a human being grows into the world and establishes a plethora of sensory relations with it. It follows that in the context of consumerism those beings that a media-driven ideological "apparatus" shapes and colonizes have to be replaced by a new concept of *citizen-subjects* who, while held together by fate and analytically militant, think about habitability through the three lenses of mental, social and environmental ecology.[3] Those who enjoy the privilege of intervening where subjectivation is at issue—theorists, educators, media people, artists, architects, urban planners, those active in sports, food or fashion and others—have a responsibility to introduce a wedge that would open a gap in the economic sphere of "official" or decreed modes of thinking. In a recent interview, Jacques Rancière (2009), former editor and co-worker with Louis Althusser, asserts that, in an age of

---

2   In her excellent *Hijacking Sustainability* (2009), Adrian Parr exposes how corporations "hijack" or appropriate ecological notions for their own profit. One does not have to agree with Slavoj Žižek (2008a; 2008b) for whom all sustainability is de facto an appropriation of ecology by capitalism.

3   I have used *apparatus* in order to recall its famous inflections, in the age of 1968, when Louis Althusser, in *For Marx* and other writings, conceived the doublet of "repressive" state apparatus and "ideological" state apparatus. The former, seen in armed forces in uniform, whether belonging to the police or the military sector, was obvious and visible to one and all. The latter, because it promoted an "imaginary relation with real modes of production," could be felt more than seen and as such belonged to schooling, intellectual life, debates over national policy and the like. So pervasive and productive were the terms that in shorthand they went by the acronyms of "RSA" and "ISA." What now comes forward is the need to locate each apparatus in the "state" where that entity is now far less visible than it had been. Could it now be said that an "IMA" or "ideological media apparatus" has taken the place of "ISA"?

construction—what he calls the "aesthetic age" in which he sees humans as living since the Revolution of 1789 (at least, we may add, in France!)—as citizens we must rethink the *lieu du politique*, that is, the locus or place of the political, as separate from economics alone. This reorientation would enable the opening of a space from which "all other manners of thinking space" can be invented, including those we have mentioned and others yet to come. While a complete separation of the politics from the economics might be chimerical, greater emphasis on the quality, extension and the presence of the ecosphere would be timely. It would favor novel ways for eco- and citizen-subjects—not only nationals—to occupy and invent the spaces in which they live. It would address questions of ecology and those pertaining to anthropological discrimination. To open such possibilities is henceforth the responsibility of spatial thinkers who have now become both mediators and translators of linguistic and cultural idioms alike.

We do well to return to Virilio's unsettling image of the new social pyramid that, even in a networked world, is far from being as anachronistic as one might think. It allows us to ask over and again what happens to those—that is, the majority of humans—who live *outside,* in a worldwide *banlieue* of sorts?[4] Where are they, and where do they go? What do they do? How do they live and die? Are they simply circulating in networks that never intersect with others that are more prosperous?[5] Since space has become the ever-shrinking "thing" that it is, both because of increased scarcity and because of its assimilation into globalized hyperspace, it is incumbent upon the theorist to think of open-ended and always flexible ways of constructing or informing responsible eco- and citizen-subjects. The task requires avoiding the pitfall of an overly universalist ambition and paying increased attention to ecological feedback in the context of the local struggles that invariably translate into global issues. The critic has to argue for the creation of habitable and sustainable milieus in the broadest sense for citizen-subjects who are not only nationals, and, as the events of the last decade have shown, for the confer-

---

4 Žižek (2008a; 2008b) states provocatively that ecological spaces cannot be opened without taking into account these excluded urban slum dwellers. For him, the main political task of the twenty-first century is the mobilization and organization of these slum dwellers. He urges a return to emancipatory discourses that would reconnect with those derived from 1968, which have been eclipsed by postmodernism and new forms of capitalism.

5 See Sam Kwinter's provocative and controversial "Notes on the Third Ecology" (2010). Kwinter makes Dehli's Dahravi slum a model of ecology in terms of employment and recycling in spite of its poverty. He also argues that slum dwellers intersect with more mainstream networks for whom they are economically vital.

ring upon the state agency and power to limit transnational corporatism.

What, we can finally ask, is the power of the writer-critic's intervention in an era where her or his influence is taken minimally and where their works are miniaturized, repertoried in the files of YouTube or available only on compact disks? Where, as Slavoj Žižek would have it, they work for and live off the very system they criticize? They can no longer function as priests, as censors or purveyors of truth to the "ordinary" public. Throughout his life, from his clinical work to his leadership of the Green Party of France, Guattari urged his readers to continually update their critical tools, while several years ago Latour (2004) chided critics for not following his advice.[6] Today, the philosopher of the history of science asserts that immutable models are history. The arrow of time does not always go forward. As the graying participants of May 1968 have begrudgingly acknowledged, true revolutions have become impossible. How are theorists to proceed and advocate transformation? Latour suggests that we ought to think of the world as *gaia* more than as a simple globe to be acted upon. His counsel takes into account the recognition that in our complicated, computerized world, which cannot exist without machines, certain ineffably complex human phenomena—for example, conversation, however passing or superficial, rife with symbolic residue and unconscious effects—and natural phenomena cannot be reduced to algorithms. A new universal question of habitability and sustainability overrides others. When faced with the scale of present world systems, if we believe in the premonition of some of the theorists we examined, a critic wonders what can be done. In the words Beckett is known to have said at the end of an exemplary life of creative ecology: *precious little* (Cixous 2007: 3–4). The critical interventions made by those studied in the pages above may be little but they remain, nonetheless, precious. Deleuze exhorted his readers to create interrupters, to pry open even the smallest of places—*vacuoles*—from which to enable other ways of thinking (1995). He also reminded them that humans had lost the world and that, to produce change, they must believe in the world again. Future spaces, he implied, have to be continually invented and reinvented, from every urban site to the state and world-space. As a result space will never again serve as a simple background against which heroic humans move. Today, in an era in which humans are said to have become a geological force,[7] in which

---

6 In François Dosse's biography of Deleuze and Guattari (2007: 610–11) Latour contributes an appreciation of the political and aesthetic impact of the work.

7 Quoting Dipesh Chakrabarty, who calls our era that of the anthropocene, Žižek notes that humans today are a "force of nature in the geological sense" (2010: 331).

populations have increased many times since the sixties, in which worlds are at war, resources often scarce and machines overtaking humans, an awareness of space as an ongoing *construction* has replaced this vision, and so has a sense of global interrelation. In the midst of the entirely new configuration noted above, we have to emphasize the need for a firm conviction that includes the force of tact and touch, in brief, for an eco-ethics and aesthetics that draw their principles from the spatial mutations the thinkers taken up in the preceding pages have discerned and addressed.[8] At stake is a critical practice based on translation, negotiation and collaboration to construct future spaces, singularly and collectively, from an infinite number of ever-changing networks. Such are this reader's theoretical musings aimed at the invention and reinvention of present and future ecological spaces.

8 In her acclaimed book *The Cost of Living* (1999), Arundhati Roy vehemently criticizes "big" projects and "big" ideas as being ecologically destructive.

Bibliography

Agamben, Giorgio (1998). *Homo Sacer: Sovereign Power and Bare Life*. Stanford, CA: Stanford University Press.

Ahearne, Jeremy (1995). *Michel de Certeau: Interpretation and Its Other*. London: Polity Press.

Althusser, Louis, Jacques Rancière, Pierre Macherey, Etienne Balibar and Roger Establet. (1965). *Lire "Le Capital"*. Paris: F. Maspéro. In English: *Reading "Capital"*. Trans. Ben Brewster. London: NLB, 1970.

Anderson, Benedict (1983). *Imagined Communities: Reflections on the Origin and Spread of Nationalism*. New York: Verso.

Ardagh, John (1968). *The New French Revolution*. New York: Harper & Row.

Armitage, John (ed.) (2000). *Paul Virilio: From Modernism to Hypermodernism and Beyond*. London: Sage.

— (ed.) (2001). *Virilio Live: Selected Interviews*. London: Sage.

— (2009). "In the Cities of the Beyond: An Interview with Paul Virilio." *Open 18*. http://www.skor.nl/article-4567-en.html (accessed November 10, 2011)

— (ed.) (2011). *Virilio Now*. Cambridge: Polity Press.

Augé, Marc (1985). *La traversée de Luxembourg, Paris: 20 juillet 1984: ethno-roman d'une journée française considérée sous l'angle des mœurs, de la théorie et du bonheur*. Paris: Hachette.

— (1986). *Un ethnologue dans le métro*. Paris: Hachette. In English: *In the Metro*. Trans. Tom Conley. Minneapolis, MN: University of Minnesota Press, 2001.

— (1994). *Le sens des autres: actualité de l'anthropologie*. Paris: Fayard. In English: *A Sense of the Other: The Timeliness and Relevance of Anthropology*. Trans. Amy Jacobs. Stanford, CA: Stanford University Press, 1998.

— (1995). *Non-Places: Introduction to an Anthropology of Supermodernity*. Trans. John Howe. London: Verso.

— (1996). "Paris and the Ethnography of the Contemporary World." In Michael Sheringham (ed.), *Parisian Fields*. London: Reaktion Books.

— (1997). *La guerre des rêves: exercises d'ethno-fiction*. Paris: Seuil.

— (1998). *Les formes de l'oubli*. Paris: Payot & Rivages.

— (2005). *La mère d'Arthur*. Paris: Fayard.

— (2006). *Le métier d'anthropologue: sens et liberté*. Paris: Galilée.

— (2007). *Casablanca*. Paris: Seuil.

— (2008). *Le métro révisité*. Paris: Seuil.

Augé, Marc, Jean Baudrillard, Daniel Bougnoux, Régis Debray, Françoise Gaillard, Edgar Morin and Salman Rushdie (1998). *Diana Crash*. Paris: Descartes.

Bachelard, Gaston (1964). *The Poetics of Space*. Trans. Maria Jolas. New York: Orion Press.

— (1983). *Water and Dreams: An Essay on the Imagination of Matter*. Trans. Edith R. Farrell. Dallas: Pegasus Foundation.

Backès-Clément, Catherine (1995). "Interview: Gilles Deleuze and Félix Guattari on Anti-Oedipus." In Gilles Deleuze (ed.), *Negotiations*. Trans. Martin Joughin. New

York: Columbia University Press. 13–24.

Baecque, Antoine de (2008). *L'histoire-caméra*. Paris: Gallimard.

Balibar, Etienne (1991). "Citizen-Subject." In Eduardo Cadava, Peter Connor and Jean-Luc Nancy (eds.), *Who Comes After the Subject?* New York: Routledge. 33–57.

— (1993). "L'Europe des citoyens." In Olivier Le Cour Grandmaison and Catherine Withol de Wenden (eds.), *Les étrangers dans la cité: expériences européennes*. Paris: La Découverte. 192–208.

— (1995). "Globalization/Cizilization I & II." Interview conducted by Jean-François Chevrier, Catherine David and Nadia Tazi. In Catherine David and Jean-François Chevrier (eds.), *Politics Poetics, Documenta X*. Kassel: Kantz. 774–99.

— (1998). *Droit de cité: culture et politique en démocratie*. Paris: Éditions de l'Aube.

— (2000). *Nous, citoyens d'Europe? Les frontières, l'état, le people*. Paris: La Découverte. In English: *We, the People of Europe? Reflections on Transnational Citizenship*. Trans. James Swensen. Princeton, NJ: Princeton University Press, 2004.

— (2003). *L'Europe, L'Amérique, la guerre: réflexions sur la médiation européenne*. Paris: La Découverte.

— (2005). *Europe constitution frontière*. Bègles: Éditions du Passant.

— (2010). "Europe is a Dead Political Project." *The Guardian*, May 25, 2010. http://www.guardian.co.uk/commentisfree/2010/may/25/eu-crisis-catastrophic-consequences?INTCMP=SRCH (accessed November 10, 2011).

Balibar, Etienne and Immanuel Wallerstein (1991). *Race, Nation, Class: Ambiguous Identities*. Trans. Chris Turner. New York: Routledge, Chapman & Hall.

Balibar, Etienne, Monique Chemillier-Gendreau, Jacqueline Costa-Lascoux and Emmanuel Terray (1999). *Sans-papiers: l'archaïsme fatal*. Paris: La Découverte.

Balibar, Etienne and Thierry Pacquot. (2001). Interview, April 6. Institut d'urbanisme de Paris, Université Paris 12, Val de Marne. http://urbanisme.u-pec.fr/documentation/paroles/etienne-balibar

Barbery, Muriel, Tahar Ben Jelloun, Alain Borer, Roland Brival, Maryse Condé, Didier Daeninckx et al. (2007). "Pour une 'littérature-monde' en français: Le manifeste de quarante-quatre écrivains en faveur d'une langue française qui serait libérée de son pacte exclusif avec la nation." *Le Monde*, March 16.

Barthes, Roland. (1957). *Mythologies*. Paris: Seuil.

Bateson, Gregory. (1972). *Steps to an Ecology of Mind*. New York: Chandler.

Baudrillard, Jean. (1983). *Simulations*. Trans. Paul Foss, Paul Patton and Philip Beitchman. New York: Semiotext(e).

— (1987). *Cool Memories*. Paris: Galilée.

— (1988). *America*. Trans. Chris Turner. New York: Verso.

— (1991). "L'Amérique ou la pensée de l'espace." In Yves Dauge (ed.), *Citoyenneté et urbanité*. Paris: Esprit/Seuil. 155–64.

— (1994). *Simulacra and Simulations*. Trans. Sheila Glaser. Ann Arbor, MI: University of Michigan Press.

— (1995). *The Gulf War Did Not Take Place*. Bloomington, IN: Indiana University Press.

— (1996). *The System of Objects*. Trans. James Benedict. New York: Verso.

— (2007). *Forget Foucault*. Trans. Nicole Dufresne. Cambridge, MA: MIT Press.

— (2009). *Why Hasn't Everything Already Disappeared?* Trans. Chris Turner. New

York: Seagull.

Beauvoir, Simone de (1966). *Les belles images*. Paris: Gallimard.

Begag, Azouz (1986). *Le gone du chaâba*. Paris: Éditions du Seuil. In English: *Shantytown Kid*. Trans. Naïma Wolf and Alec G. Hargreaves. Lincoln, NE: University of Nebraska Press, 2007.

— (1989). "North African Immigrants in France: The Socio-Spatial Representation of 'Here' and 'There.'" Loughborough, UK: University of Loughborough European Research Center.

— (1991). *La ville des autres: la famille immigrée et l'espace urbain*. Lyon. Presses Universitaires de Lyon.

— (1994). *Quartiers sensibles*. Paris: Seuil.

— (1995). *Espace et exclusion: mobilitiés dans les quartiers périphériques d'Avignon*. Paris: L'Harmattan.

Bégaudeau, François (2009). *The Class*. Trans. Linda Asher. New York: Seven Stories Press.

Benjamin, Walter (1999). "Paris, Capital of the Nineteenth Century." In *The Arcades Project*. Trans. Howard Eiland and Kevin McLoughlin. Cambridge, MA: Belknap Press of Harvard University Press.

Benko, G. and Ulf Strohmeyer (eds.) (1997). *Space and Social Theory: Interpreting Modernity and Postmodernity*. Oxford: Blackwell.

Backstein, Joseph, Daniel Birnbaum and Sven-Olov Wallenstein (eds.) (2008). *Thinking Worlds: The Moscow Conference on Philosophy, Politics and Art*. Berlin and Moscow: Sternberg Press and Interros Publishing.

Bishop, Ryan (ed.) (2009). *Baudrillard Now*. Cambridge: Polity Press.

Bois, Yves-Alain (1994). "French Lib." In Denis Hollier (ed.), *A New History of French Literature*. Cambridge, MA: Harvard University Press. 1040–45.

Bridge, Gary and Sophie Watson (2002). *The Blackwell City Reader*. Malden, MA: Blackwell Publishers.

Buchanan, Ian (2000). *Michel de Certeau: Cultural Theorist*. London: Sage.

Buchanan, Ian and Gregg Lambert (eds.) (2005). *Deleuze and Space*. Toronto: University of Toronto Press.

Buchanan, Ian and Adrian Parr (eds.) (2006). *Deleuze in the Contemporary World*. Edinburgh: Edinburgh University Press.

Casey, Edward S. (1997). *The Fate of Place: A Philosophical History*. Berkeley, CA: University of California Press.

Castells, Manuel (1972). *La question urbaine*. Paris: F. Maspero.

— (1979). *The Urban Question: A Marxist Approach*. Trans. Alan Sheridan. Cambridge, MA: MIT Press.

— (1983). *The City and the Grassroots: A Cross-Cultural Theory of Urban Social Movements*. Berkeley, CA: University of California Press.

— (1996). *The Rise of the Network Society. The Information Age: Economy, Society and Culture Vol. 1*. Cambridge, MA: Blackwell Publishers.

— (1997). *The Power of Identity. The Information Age: Economy, Society and Culture Vol. 2*. Cambridge, MA: Blackwell Publishers.

— (1998). *End of Millennium. The Information Age: Economy, Society and Culture Vol. 3*. Cambridge, MA: Blackwell Publishers.

Centre de Création Industrielle (1979). *Alternances urbaines*. Paris: Centre Georges Pompidou/CCI.

Certeau, Michel de (1982). *La Fable mystique: XVIe—XVIIe siècle*. Paris: Gallimard.
— (1984). *The Practice of Everyday Life*. Trans. Steven Rendell. Berkeley, CA: University of California Press.
— (1986). *Heterologies: Discourse on the Other*. Trans. Brian Massumi. Minneapolis, MN: University of Minnesota Press.
— (1988). *The Writing of History*. Trans. Tom Conley. New York: Columbia University Press.
— (1997a). *The Capture of Speech and Other Political Writings*. Trans. Tom Conley. Minneapolis, MN: University of Minnesota Press.
— (1997b). *Culture in the Plural*. Trans. Tom Conley. Minneapolis, MN: University of Minnesota Press.
Certeau, Michel de, Dominique Julia and Jacques Revel (1975). *Une politique de la langue: la Révolution française et les patois: l'enquête de Grégoire*. Paris: Gallimard.
Certeau, Michel de, Luce Giard and Pierre Mayol (1998). *The Practice of Everyday Life. Volume 2: Living and Cooking*. Trans. Timothy J. Tomasik. Minneapolis, MN: University of Minnesota Press.
Cesbron, Gilbert (1954). *Chiens perdus sans collier*. Paris: J. Tallandier.
Chakrabarty, Dipesh (2009). "The Climate of History: Four Theses." *Critical Inquiry* 35.2. 197–202.
Charef, Mehdi (1983). *Le thé au harem d'Archi Ahmed*. Paris: Mercure de France.
Citton, Yves (2008). "Esquisse d'une économie politique des affects." In Yves Citton and Frédéric Lordon (eds.), *Spinoza et les sciences sociales. De la puissance de la multitude à l'économie des affects*. Paris: Editions Amsterdam.
— (2010a). *Mythocratie: Storytelling et imaginaire de gauche*. Paris: Éditions Amsterdam.
— (2010b). *Zazirocratie*. Paris: Editions Amsterdam.
Cixous, Hélène (1998). *Stigmata: Escaping Texts*. New York: Routledge.
— (2007). *Le Voisin de zero: Sam Beckett*. Paris: Galilée.
Clifford, James and George E. Marcus (eds.) (1986). *Writing Culture: The Poetics and Politics of Ethnography: A School of American Research Advanced Seminar*. Berkeley, CA: University of California Press.
Coloma, Tristan (2010). "L'improbable saga des Africains en Chine: Travailleurs immigrés menaces d'expulsion." *Le monde diplomatique*, 1 May. 12–13.
Comolli, Jean-Louis (2009). *Cinéma contre spectacle*. Paris: Editions Verdier.
Conley, Dalton (2009). *Elsewhere, U.S.A*. New York: Pantheon Books.
Conley, Verena Andermatt (ed.) (1993). *Rethinking Technologies*. Minneapolis, MN: University of Minnesota Press.
— (1997). *Ecopolitics: The Environment in Poststructuralist Thought*. New York: Routledge.
— (2003). *The War against the Beavers: Learning to be Wild in the Northwoods*. Minneapolis, MN: University of Minnesota Press.
— (2010a). "Literature, Space and the French Nation-State after the 1960s." In Christie McDonald and Susan Suleiman (eds.), *French Global*. New York: Columbia University Press. 145–59.
— (2010b). "Negotiating Space in Post-68 French Thought." *Hagar: Studies in Culture, Polity and Identities* 10.1 (special issue on *The Spatial Turn in Social Theory*. Ed. Yishai Blank and Issi Rosen-Zvi). 9–22.

Crang, Mike and Nigel Thrift (eds.) (2000). *Thinking Space*. New York: Routledge.

Cusset, François (2008). *French Theory: How Foucault, Derrida, Deleuze, & Co. Transformed the Intellectual Life of the United States*. Trans. Jeff Fort. Minneapolis, MN: University of Minnesota Press.

Deleuze, Gilles (1963). *La philosophie critique de Kant: doctrine des facultés*. Paris: Presses Universitaires de France.

— (1983). *L'image-mouvement*. Paris: Editions de Minuit. In English: *The Movement Image*. Trans. Hugh Tomlinson and Robert Galeta. Minneapolis, MN: University of Minnesota Press, 1989.

— (1985). *L'image-temps*. Paris: Éditions de Minuit. In English: *The Time Image*. Trans. Hugh Tomlinson and Barbara Habberjam. Minneapolis, MN: University of Minnesota Press, 2005.

— (1986). *Foucault*. Paris: Éditions de Minuit.

— (1988). *Le Pli: Leibniz et le baroque*. Paris: Editions de Minuit. In English: *The Fold: Leibniz and the Baroque*. Trans. Tom Conley. Minneapolis, MN: University of Minnesota Press, 1993.

— (1992). "L'épuisé." In Samuel Beckett, *Quad*. Paris: Éditions de Minuit.

— (1995). "Postscript on the Societies of Control." In Gilles Deleuze (ed.), *Negotiations*. Trans. Martin Joughin. New York: Columbia University Press.

Deleuze, Gilles and Félix Guattari (1977). *Anti-Oedipus: Capitalism and Schizophrenia*. Trans. Robert Hurley, Mark Seem and Helen R. Lane. New York: Viking Press.

— (1987). *A Thousand Plateaus: Capitalism and Schizophrenia*. Trans. Brian Massumi. Minneapolis, MN: University of Minnesota Press.

— (1994). *What is Philosophy?* Trans. Hugh Tomlinson and Graham Burchell. New York: Columbia University Press.

Depardon, Raymond and Paul Virilio (2008). *Native Land: Stop Eject*. Paris: Fondation Cartier pour l'art contemporain.

Derrida, Jacques (1995). *Mal d'archive: une impression freudienne*. Paris: Galilée.

— (2003). *Voyous: deux essais sur la raison*. Paris: Galilée. In English: *Rogues: Two Essays on Reason*. Trans. Pascal-Anne Brault and Michael Nass. Stanford, CA: Stanford University Press, 2005.

Descartes, René (1996). *Meditations on First Philosophy: With Selections from the Objections and Replies*. Trans. John Cottingham. Cambridge: Cambridge University Press.

Doel, Marcus (1999). *Poststructuralist Geographies*. Edinburgh: Edinburgh University Press.

Dosse, François (2002). *Michel de Certeau: le marcheur blessé*. Paris: La Découverte.

— (2007). *Gilles Deleuze et Félix Guattari: biographie croisée*. Paris: La Découverte.

Ethridge, Roe (2007). "Regime Change: Jacques Rancière and Contemporary Art." *Art Forum International*, March 1.

European Council of Town Planners (2003). *The New Charter of Athens 2003: The European Council of Town Planners' Vision for Cities in the 21st Century*. Lisbon.

Farinelli, Franco (2009). *De la raison cartographique*. Trans. Katia Bienvenu in collaboration with Brice Gruet. Paris: CTHS.

Featherstone, Mike, Nigel Thrift and John Urry (eds.) (2005). *Automobilities*. London: Sage.

Foucault, Michel (1977). *Discipline and Punish: The Birth of the Prison*. Trans. Alan

Sheridan. New York: Pantheon Books.

— (1984). "Des espaces autres." *Architecture, Mouvement, Continuité* 5 (October). 46–49. In English: "Of Other Spaces." Trans. Jay Miskowiec. *Diacritics* 16 (Spring 1986). 22–27.

Friedman, Thomas (2005). *The World is Flat: A Brief History of the Twenty-First Century.* New York: Farrar, Straus & Giroux.

— (2008). *Hot, Flat, and Crowded: Why We Need a Green Revolution, and How it Can Renew America.* New York: Farrar, Straus & Giroux.

Goody, Jack (1977). *The Domestication of the Savage Mind.* Cambridge: Cambridge University Press.

Goonewardena, Kanishka, Stefan Kipfer, Richard Milgrom and Christian Schmid (eds.) (2008). *Space, Difference, Everyday Life: Reading Henri Lefebvre.* New York: Routledge.

Guattari, Félix (1984). *Molecular Revolution: Psychiatry and Politics.* Trans. Rosemary Sheed. New York: Penguin.

— (1995). *Chaosmosis: An Ethico-Aesthetic Paradigm.* Trans. Paul Bains and Julian Pefanis. Bloomington, IN: Indiana University Press.

— (2000). *The Three Ecologies.* Trans. Ian Pindar and Paul Sutton. London: Athlone.

— (2004). "Vers une ère postmedia." http://multitudes.samizdat.net/Vers-une-ere-postmedia (accessed November 10, 2011).

— (2008). "Du postmoderne au postmédia." *Multitudes* 34. 128–33.

Hardt, Michael and Antonio Negri (2000). *Empire.* Cambridge, MA: Harvard University Press.

— (2004). *Multitude: War and Democracy in the Age of Empire.* New York: Penguin.

— (2009). *Commonwealth.* Cambridge, MA: Belknap Press of Harvard University Press.

Harvey, David (2000). *Spaces of Hope.* Berkeley, CA: University of California Press.

— (2006). *Spaces of Global Capitalism: Towards a Theory of Uneven Geographical Development.* London: Verso.

— (2009a). *Cosmopolitanism and the Geographies of Freedom.* New York; Columbia University Press

— (2009b). *Social Justice and the City.* Rev. edn. Athens, GA: University of Georgia Press.

— (2012). *From the Right to the City to the Urban Revolution.* New York: Verso.

Heidegger, Martin (1993). "Building Dwelling Thinking." In David Farrell Krell (ed.), *Basic Writings: From Being and Time (1927) to The Task of Thinking (1964).* San Francisco: Harper San Francisco.

Herzogenrath, Bernd (ed.). (2009). *Deleuze/Guattari & Ecology.* New York: Palgrave Macmillan.

Highmore, Ben (2002). *Everyday Life and Cultural Theory.* New York: Routledge.

Hollier, Denis (1982). *Politique de la prose: Sartre et l'an quarante: essai.* Paris: Gallimard.

Huntington, Samuel P. (1997). *The Clash of Civilizations and the Remaking of World Order.* New York: Touchstone.

Huyssen, Andreas (ed.) (2008). *Other Cities, Other Worlds: Urban Imaginaries in a Globalizing Age.* Durham, NC: Duke University Press.

Jameson, Fredric (1991). *Postmodernism, or, The Cultural Logic of Late Capitalism.* Durham, NC: Duke University Press.

Kassovitz, Mathieu (1995). *Jusqu'ici tout va bien: scenario et photographies autour du film La haine.* Arles: Actes Sud.

Kellner, Douglas (1994). *Baudrillard: A Critical Reader.* Cambridge: Blackwell Publishers.

— (2005). *Media Spectacle and the Crisis of Democracy.* Boulder, CO: Paradigm Publishers.

Kittler, Friedrich and Paul Virilio (2001). "The Information Bomb: A Conversation." In John Armitage (ed.), *Virilio Live: Selected Interviews.* London: Sage.

Koolhaas, Rem (1978). *Delirious New York: A Retroactive Manifesto for Manhattan.* New York: Oxford University Press.

Kwinter, Sanford (2010). "Notes on the Third Ecology." In Moshen Mostafavi and Gareth Doherty (eds.), *Ecological Urbanism: Alternative and Sustainable Cities of the Future.* Baden: Lars Müller Publishers. 94–105.

Laferrière, Dany (2006). *Vers le sud.* Paris: Grasset.

Latour, Bruno (1999). "On Recalling ANT." In John Law and John Hassard (eds.), *Actor Network and After.* Oxford: Blackwell Publishers and the Sociological Review. 15–25.

— (2002). *War of the Worlds: What About Peace?* Trans. Charlotte Bigg. Chicago: Prickly Paradigm Press.

— (2004). "Why has Critique Run out of Steam? From Matters of Fact to Matters of Concern." *Critical Inquiry* 30.2. 225–48.

— (2005). *Reassembling the Social: An Introduction to Actor-Network Theory.* Oxford: Oxford University Press.

— (2009). "Spheres and Networks: Two Ways to Reinterpret Globalization." *Harvard Design Magazine* 30 (Spring/Summer). 138–44.

— (2010). "Forty Years Later: Back to a Sub-lunar Earth." In Moshen Mostafavi and Gareth Doherty (eds.) *Ecological Urbanism: Alternative and Sustainable Cities of the Future.* Baden: Lars Müller Publishers. 124–29.

Latour, Bruno and Emilie Hermant (1998). *Paris: ville invisible.* Paris: La Découverte.

Latour, Bruno, Emilie Hermant and Patricia Reed. *Paris: Invisible City.* Text: Bruno Latour. Photos: Emilie Hermant. Trans. Liz Carey-Libbrecht. Web design: Patricia Reed. www.bruno-latour.fr/virtual/paris/english/frames.html (accessed February 3, 2012).

Latour, Bruno and Peter Weibel (eds.) (2002). *Iconoclash: Beyond the Image Wars in Science, Religion and Art.* Cambridge, MA: MIT Press.

— (eds.) (2005). *Making Things Public: Atmospheres of Democracy.* Trans. Robert Bryce. Cambridge, MA: MIT Press.

Leach, Neil (ed.) (1992). *Rethinking Architecture: A Reader in Cultural Theory.* New York: Routledge.

Lefebvre, Henri (1947). *Critique de la vie quotidienne 1: Introduction.* Paris: Grasset.

— (1970) *La révolution urbaine.* Paris: Gallimard.

— (1974). *La production de l'espace.* Paris: Éditions Anthropos.

— (1991a). *Critique of Everyday Life.* Trans. John Moore. New York: Verso.

— (1991b). *The Production of Space.* Trans. Donald Nicholson-Smith. Cambridge, MA: Blackwell Publishers.

— (1992). *Eléments de rythmanalyse.* Paris: Éditions Syllepse.

— (1996). *Writings on Cities.* Ed. and Trans. Eleonor Kofman and Elizabeth Lebas. Cambridge, MA: Blackwell Publishers.

— (2003). *The Urban Revolution.* Trans. Robert Bononno. Minneapolis, MN: University of Minnesota Press.

— (2004). *Rhythmanalysis: Space, Time and Everyday Life.* Trans. Stuart Elden and Gerald Moore. New York: Continuum.

— (2009a). *Dialectical Materialism.* Trans. John Sturrock. Minneapolis, MN: University of Minnesota Press.

— (2009b). *State, Space, World: Selected Essays.* Ed. Neil Brenner and Stuart Elden. Trans. Gerald Moore, Neil Brenner and Stuart Elden. Minneapolis, MN: University of Minnesota Press.

Leuwers, Daniel (ed.) (1984). *Arthur Rimbaud: Poésies complètes.* Paris: Librairie Générale Française.

Lévi-Strauss, Claude (1955). *Tristes tropiques.* Paris: Plon.

Lotringer, Sylvère and Paul Virilio (2008). *Pure War.* Trans. Mark Polizzotti and Brian O'Keeffe. New York: Semiotext(e).

Magatti, Mauro and Laura Gherardi (eds.) (2009). *The City of Flows: Territories, Agencies and Institutions.* Milan: Bruno Mondadori.

Maspéro, François (1994). *Roissy Express: A Journey Through the Paris Suburbs.* Trans. Paul Jones. New York: Verso.

Mauss, Marcel (1950). *Sociologie et anthropologie.* Paris: Presses Universitaires de France.

— (2002). *The Gift: The Form and Reason for Exchange in Archaic Societies.* New York and London: Routledge.

Memmi, Albert (1957). *Portrait du colonisé: précédé du portrait du colonisateur.* Paris: Buchet/Chastel. In English: *The Colonizer and the Colonized.* Trans. Howard Greenfield. London: Earthscan, 2003.

— (2004). *Portrait du décolonisé arabo-musulman et de quelques autres.* Paris: Gallimard. In English: *Decolonization and the Decolonized.* Trans. Robert Bononno. Minneapolis, MN: University of Minnesota Press, 2006.

Merchant, Carolyn (1978). *The Death of Nature.* Berkeley, CA: University of California Press.

Morton, Timothy (2005). *Ecology without Nature: Rethinking Environmental Aesthetics.* Cambridge, MA: Harvard University Press.

Mostafavi, Mohsen and Gareth Doherty (eds.) (2010). *Ecological Urbanism: Alternative and Sustainable Cities of the Future.* Baden: Lars Müller Publishers.

Mumford, Lewis (1961). *The City in History: Its Origins, Its Transformations and Its Prospects.* New York: Harcourt, Brace & World.

— (1970). *The Culture of Cities.* New York: Harcourt, Brace & Jovanovich.

Nancy, Jean-Luc (1993). *Le sens du monde.* Paris: Galilée. In English: *The Sense of the World.* Trans. Jeffrey S. Librett. Minneapolis, MN: University of Minnesota Press, 1997.

Parr, Adrian (2009). *Hijacking Sustainability.* Cambridge, MA: MIT Press.

Parr, Adrian and Michael Zaretsky (eds.) (2011). *New Directions In Sustainable Design.* New York: Routledge.

Perec, Georges (1965). *Les choses: une histoire des années soixante.* Paris: Julliard. In English: *Things: A Story of the Sixties.* Trans. David Bellos. Boston: D. Godine, 1990.

— (1997). *Species of Spaces and Other Pieces.* Trans. John Sturrock. New York: Penguin.

Poster, Mark (ed.) (2001). *Jean Baudrillard*. Stanford, CA: Stanford University Press.

— (2006). *Information Please: Culture and Politics in the Age of Digital Machines*. Durham, NC: Duke University Press.

Poster, Mark and David Savat (eds.) (2009). *Deleuze and New Technology*. Edinburgh: Edinburgh University Press.

Rancière, Jacques (1995). *La mésentente: politique et philosophie*. Paris: Galilée.

— (2000). *Le partage du sensible: esthétique et politique*. Paris: Galilée. In English: *The Politics of Aesthetics: The Distribution of the Sensible*. Trans. Gabriel Rockhill. New York: Continuum, 2004.

— (2004). *Malaise dans l'esthétique*. Paris: Galilée. In English: *Aesthetics and its Discontents*. Trans. Steven Corcoran. Cambridge: Polity Press, 2009.

— (2005). *La haine de la démocratie*. Paris: Fabrique.

— (2009). *Et tant pis pour les gens fatigues: Entretiens*. Paris: Éditions Amsterdam.

Rancière, Jacques and Fulvia Carnevale (2007). "The Art of the Possible: Jacques Rancière in Conversation with Fulvia Carnevale and John Kelsey." *Artforum*, March. 256–69.

Redhead, Steve (2004). *Paul Virilio: Theorist for an Accelerated Culture*. Edinburgh: Edinburgh University Press.

Ricardou, Jean (1971). *Révolutions minuscules*. Paris: Gallimard.

Rockhill, Gabriel and Pierre-Antoine Chardel (eds.) (2009). *Technologies de contrôle dans la mondialisation: enjeux politiques, éthiques et esthétiques*. Paris: Kimé.

Ross, Kristin (1995). *Fast Cars, Clean Bodies: Decolonization and the Reordering of French Culture*. Cambridge, MA: MIT Press.

— (2007). "Kristin Ross on Jacques Rancière." *Art Forum International*, March 1.

Roy, Arundhati (1999). *The Cost of Living*. New York: Modern Library.

Rushdie, Salman (1988). *The Satanic Verses*. London: Viking.

Sassen, Saskia (1991). *The Global City: New York, London, Tokyo*. Princeton, NJ: Princeton University Press.

Simondon, Gilbert (1958). *Du mode d'existence des objects techniques*. Paris: Éditions Aubier-Montaigne.

Soja, Edward W. (1989). *Postmodern Geographies: The Reassertion of Space in Critical Social Theory*. New York: Verso.

— (1996). *Thirdspace: Journey to Los Angeles and Other Real-and-Imagined Places*. Cambridge, MA: Blackwell Publishers.

— (2010). *Seeking Spatial Justice*. Minneapolis, MN: University of Minnesota Press.

Starr, Peter (1995). *Logics of a Failed Revolt: French Theory After May '68*. Stanford, CA: Stanford University Press.

Stengers, Isabelle (2002). *Sciences et pouvoirs: la démocratie face à la technoscience*. Paris: La Découverte.

— (2003a). *Cosmopolitiques I: La guerre des sciences; L'invention de la mécanique: pouvoir et raison; Thermodynamique: la réalité physique en crise*. Paris: La Découverte.

— (2003b). *Cosmopolitiques II: Mécanique quantique: la fin du rêve; Au nom de la flèche du temps: le défi de Prigogine; La vie et l'artifice: visages de l'émergence*. Paris: La Découverte.

— (2010). *Cosmopolitics*, vol. 1. Trans. Robert Bononno. Minneapolis: University of Minnesota Press.

Stiegler, Bernard and Frédéric Neyrat (2006). "Interview: De l'économie libidinale à l'écologie de l'esprit." *Multitudes* 24. 85–95.

Taylor, Astra (2009). *Examined Life: Excursions with Eight Contemporary Thinkers*. Cambridge: New Press.

Thrift, Nigel. (2002). "Driving in the City." In Gary Bridge and Sophie Waters (eds.), *The Blackwell City Reader*. Malden, MA: Wiley-Blackwell. 152–58.

— (2008). *Non-representational Theory: Space, Politics, Affect*. London: Routledge.

Trebitsch, Michael (1991). "Preface." In Henri Lefebvre, *Critique of Everyday Life*. Trans. John Moore. New York: Verso. ix–xxviii.

Vattimo, Gianni and Pier Aldo Rovatti (eds.) (1988). *Il pensiero debole*. Milan: Feltrinelli.

Virilio, Paul (1977). "Métempsychose du passager." *Traverses* 8. 11–19.

— (1978). *Défense populaire et luttes écologiques*. Paris: Galilée.

— (1980). *Esthétique de la disparition*. Paris: Bolland. In English: *Aesthetics of Disappearance*. Trans. Philip Beitchman. New York: Semiotext(e).

— (1984). *L'espace critique: essai*. Paris: Bourgois.

— (1986). *Speed and Politics: An Essay on Dromology*. Trans. Mark Polizzotti. New York: Columbia University Press.

— (1990). *Popular Defense and Ecological Struggles*. Trans. Mark Polizzotti. New York: Semiotext(e).

— (1991). *The Lost Dimension*. Trans. Daniel Moshenberg. New York: Semiotext(e).

— (1993). "The Third Interval: A Critical Transition." In Verena Andermatt Conley (ed.), *Rethinking Technologies*. Minneapolis, MN: University of Minnesota Press. 3–12.

— (1994). *Bunker Archeology: Texts and Photos*. Trans. George Collins. New York: Princeton Architectural Press.

— (1995). *The Art of the Motor*. Trans. Julie Rose. Minneapolis, MN: University of Minnesota Press.

— (1999). *Cyberworld: The Politics of the Very Worst: Conversation with Philippe Petit*. New York: Semiotext(e).

— (2000a). *The Information Bomb*. Trans. Chris Turner. New York: Verso.

— (2000b). *Strategies of Deception*. Trans. Chris Turner. New York: Verso.

— (2005a). *City of Panic*. Trans. Julie Rose. New York: Berg.

— (2005b). *Open Sky*. Trans. Julie Rose. New York: Verso.

— (2008). "Une anthropologie du pressentiment." In Jean-Paul Colleyn and Jean-Pierre Dozon (eds.), *L'Anthropologie et le contemporain: Autour de Marc Augé*, *L'Homme*, 185–86. 97–104.

— (2009). *Le futurisme de l'instant: stop-eject*. Paris: Galilée.

— (2010). *Futurism of the Instant: Stop-Eject*. Trans. Julie Rose. Oxford: Polity Press.

Williams, Raymond (1958). *Culture and Society: 1780–1950*. New York: Columbia University Press.

— (1999). *The Country and the City Revisited: England and the Politics of Culture*, *1550–1850*. Ed. Gerald MacLean, Donna Landry and Joseph P. Ward. New York: Columbia University Press.

Yaari, Monique (2008). *Rethinking the French City: Architecture, Dwelling and Display after 1968*. Amsterdam: Rodopi.

Žižek, Slavoj (2008a). "Nature and Its Discontents." *Substance* 117.37.3. 37–72.

— (2008b). *In Defense of Lost Causes*. London: Verso.

— (2008c). "Censorship Today: Violence or Ecology as a New Opium for the Masses." www.lacan.com/zizecology1.htm.

— (2009). "Ecology." Conversation with Astra Taylor. In Astra Taylor, *Examined Life: Excursions with Eight Contemporary Thinkers*. Cambridge: New Press. 155–83.

— (2010). *Living in the End Times*. New York: Verso.

Index

Printed and bound by CPI Group (UK) Ltd, Croydon, CR0 4YY

25/03/2025

14647349-0005